ROUTLEDGE LIBRARY EDITIONS:
GROUP THERAPY

Volume 8

HOW TO BEGIN A PSYCHOTHERAPY GROUP

HOW TO BEGIN A PSYCHOTHERAPY GROUP

Six Approaches

Edited by
HERBERT M. RABIN AND MAX ROSENBAUM

Routledge
Taylor & Francis Group
LONDON AND NEW YORK

First published in 1976

This edition first published in 2015
by Routledge
27 Church Road, Hove BN3 2FA

and by Routledge
711 Third Avenue, New York, NY 10017

Routledge is an imprint of the Taylor & Francis Group, an informa business

British Library Cataloguing in Publication Data
A catalogue record for this book is available from the British Library

ISBN: 978-1-138-79428-3 (Set)
eISBN: 978-1-315-74758-3 (Set)
ISBN: 978-1-138-80139-4 (Volume 8)
eISBN: 978-1-315-75461-1 (Volume 8)

Publisher's Note
The publisher has gone to great lengths to ensure the quality of this reprint but points out that some imperfections in the original copies may be apparent.

Disclaimer
The publisher has made every effort to trace copyright holders and would welcome correspondence from those they have been unable to trace.

HOW TO BEGIN A PSYCHOTHERAPY GROUP: SIX APPROACHES

Edited by

HERBERT M. RABIN

and

MAX ROSENBAUM

GORDON AND BREACH SCIENCE PUBLISHERS

London New York Paris

Editorial office for the United States of America
Gordon and Breach Science Publishers, Inc.
One Park Avenue
New York, N.Y. 10016

Editorial office for France
Gordon and Breach
7–9 rue Emile Dubois
Paris 75014

This title was first available to the reading public in *Group Process* (Vol. 7, No. 1).

Library of Congress catalog card number 76-13292 ISBN 0 677 15800 9 (*cloth*). Printed in Great Britain by W. & G. Baird Ltd. (Northern Ireland).

CONTENTS

From the editor

This collection of articles is the result of much hard work by HERBERT RABIN, who served as cooperating editor for the book. His interest in how different experts approach the formation and beginning of a psychotherapy group has "paid off" in a way that we hope will be of interest to our readers. Since we did not expect to get the manuscripts, when they ended up in our hands we jumped at the opportunity to present the different points of view. We hope you like the result.

MAX ROSENBAUM

How to begin a psychotherapy group: six approaches

HERBERT M. RABIN

INTRODUCTION

BEGINNINGS have always fascinated man. How did the world begin? How did plant and animal life evolve? How does each human life develop from the moment of conception? Beginnings—beginnings of ideas, of romance, of wars, intrigue us.

Beginnings are vital. If we tend a sapling tree with the appropriate soil, fertilizer, shade, water, etc., a strong, healthy, durable tree will probably develop. If however, we make one or two serious omissions or mistakes in planting and early care, our sampling tree will develop weak and stunted; it may even die before fully living. Then, no later intervention, however intelligent and dramatic, may be sufficient to overcome its inadequate beginnings.

So too with a psychotherapy group. Too little thinking about or faulty preparation before and in the beginning of a therapy group can lead to serious problems—immediately or weeks later, at times even including the premature death of the group. On the other hand, thoughtful planning of how to form the group and of how to guide the group's early development can have powerful effects, leading to an exciting, cohesive and beneficial group.

How then can we plan the beneficial therapeutic group? From years of practicing and teaching group psychotherapy, I have developed seventeen sets of issues significant to forming and beginning groups, whether psychoanalytic or psychodramatic, whether in a hospital or in a private practice setting. These issues are in the form of questions of a clinical, practical and theoretical nature. Each author has considered these ideas, and where relevant and important to his approach, discusses them.

The issues to consider in forming and beginning psychotherapy are described below.

a) What are the ideal criteria for selecting patients for your groups? How far from your ideal are you willing to deviate in actual practice? On what basis do you reject a patient from entering your groups and refer to another group? Under what conditions do you reject a patient from all groups?

b) What is your conception of the ideal composition of patients in a group? Again, how far from this ideal are you willing to deviate?

c) How do you typically prepare patients for the group? What is the usual time expenditure? How do you tell that a particular person is not ready to enter group? Then how do you work with that person?

d) What kind of contract (implicit or explicit) do you develop with the individual patient and with the group? What is the process for deriving the contract? What limits are typical? What is your position on social-personal contact between participants outside of the group? If you are writing about groups in an institution, how are your organization's needs (e.g. of immediate superior, department head, institutional philosophy, financial, etc.) reflected in your contract?

e) What is the typical description of your groups? Consider size, age, gender, socio-economic status, ethnic composition, sources of referral, description diagnosis, the patient's stated reasons for treatment, past history of individual therapy, past hospitalizations, plus any other factor you consider pertinent.

f) How do you usually administer your group? Where does the group meet (e.g. private office, hospital, college lounge, etc.)? What is the physical set-up (room shape and size, chairs and spacing, open or something in the center, usually sit on chairs or floor)? What is the frequency and duration of group meetings?

g) What is your policy of combining the group therapeutic experience with individual therapy simultaneously? What is your theoretical and clinical rationale?

h) What is your position (theoretical and practical) on co-therapists (co-equal and assistant) and observers?

i) What are your policies re: fees? If you make exceptions to the regular fee, on what basis is it determined? How and by whom is billing and collecting handled? How do you handle late payments?

j) How do you conceive of the broad strokes of the development of group phenomena over the life span of the group? Paint in some of the basic details of group development from the first session to the middle of the group life.

k) How do you conceptualize your ideal therapeutic relationship both with individual participants and the group 'as a whole'? Does this change from the first session to the middle of the group's existence? What do you see as your prime verbal and non-verbal operations as a leader? How do you work with your real, authentic self as well as transference reactions to you?

l) What are the necessary and sufficient conditions for constructive personality change to occur within the group? How do you relate this to your role described above?

m) What are some of the important DON'TS during the formation and beginning processes of the group? These are the warnings that you believe are crucial to communicate to those leading their first or second group.

n) How do you deal with the difficult patient in the preparatory and beginning phases of group? This could include: the patient with inadequate motivation for treatment; the monopolizer; the person who has a history of very destructive acting out; the patient who is very scared of group, etc.

o) What do you believe to be one or two of the most significant theoretical contributions of your approach? What are one or two of the most important clinical contributions of your approach?

p) What do you believe are one or two significant deficiencies or limitations in your approach—theoretically? Clinically?

q) Where is group therapy going—i.e. your fantasies of the future as to how your particular approach may fit into the emerging mental health field of 1980, and of 2000? Fantastic fantasies as well as thoughtful extrapolations are welcome.

The six papers that follow in this journal all focus their energies on the forming and beginning of psychotherapy groups. However, within this focus the papers cover an extremely broad range: three basic approaches (psychoanalytic, group centered, and psychodramatic), two homogeneous symptom groups (homosexual and alcoholic) and one very difficult clinical challenge (short term hospitalized groups). Each of the six authors, who are outstanding in their area of writing, will be introduced more formally in the "About The Authors" page and informally in my Editor's Note to each paper.

Cooperating editor's note

I HAVE KNOWN Max Rosenbaum for several years, the last couple of years more closely, both as friend and colleague. As a human being, Max illustrates the qualities of integrated, mature living which he espouses as "the most important point in all training." As a professional, Max is one of the leading analytic group therapists, trainers, and therapist's therapist.

This article, which is clearly written and full of salient clinical knowledge, is warmed by Max's personal examples. His more lengthy discussions of the "alternate meeting" and "selection and suitability" I found especially packed with useful ideas.

The practice and theory described in this paper is a good representation of many other experienced analytic group therapists in this country and especially in the New York City area. However, Max does deviate from my reading of "the norm" in two major ways. One, his groups meet twice weekly, as compared to the usual once a week. Secondly, whereas Max is typically opposed to combining regular individual therapy with group therapy, most experienced practitioners that I know find combined therapy very fruitful for many patients.

HERBERT RABIN

The psychoanalytic group: formation and beginnings

MAX ROSENBAUM

ROSENBAUM has defined group psychotherapy in his text on group therapy and has pointed to the continuum of group psychotherapy. The continuum ranges from the reparative and supportive approach to the reconstructive approach, which moves toward the concept of deep-seated personality change. The thrust of this chapter will be with the psychoanalytic group. There is so much distortion on the current scene as to what is psychoanalytic that certain basics must be set forth. Sigmund Freud defined psychoanalysis as any method based on the delineation of transferences and resistances. This writer would prefer to include the systematic exploration of the unconscious. We are engaged in a therapy which uncovers and reconstructs. For certain types of patients there may be modifications of technique—active intervention, for example, in the effort to get the patient to relate. But this does not take away from the fundamental concepts of what makes for psychoanalytic group therapy and this means exploration of the unconscious, analysis of transference and working through of transference reactions, and analysis and working through of resistance. While there may be some disagreements amongst group therapists who are trained in different psychoanalytic traditions, e.g., a graduate of the Karen Horney Institute, the American Institute of Psychonalysis—as opposed to a graduate of the New York Medical College Psychoanalytic Training Program, there is fundamental agreement, in my opinion, among well-trained group therapists. The techniques that they use in common far outweigh different emphases that may arise at different times. Probably the most important point in all training, whether it be the individual or group approach to psychoanalytic psychotherapy, is the personal maturity of the therapist. A happy, functioning human being who is a psychotherapist communicates a quality of integrated living in his therapeutic approach and this is particularly noted in the group run along psychoanalytic lines.

Currently there are people who assume that a meeting of three or more persons who come together at the same time and place rather regularly and talk about problems may fall under the rubric of depth group therapy. Probably there is some kind of therapy taking place, particularly if the group leader is psychoanalytically trained, but the therapy is generally quite unplanned and is really nontherapeutic group interaction. The emphasis is not on deep-seated personality change, but some kind of minimal personality alteration with an emphasis on acquiring a new behavioral repertoire for human interaction. This is *not* the intensive psychotherapeutic group.

THE NUMBER OF PATIENTS

The intensive psychotherapeutic group consists of a small number of patients, generally seven to ten in number. The size of the group has been arrived at by clinical experience. While there are some gifted group leaders who appear able to follow the currents at work in a group larger than ten in number, this appears to be unusual. The lower limit of seven is used to account for attrition, illness, and a variety of other circumstances. When a group falls below seven in number, unless it is a group that has been meeting for a long time, there is less interaction and the group seems to become rather static. About twenty years ago I became intrigued as to why groups seemed to function best when there were ten in number equally distributed between men and women. I spent many hours with theologians and anthropologists, beginning with theories related to fingers of the hands (ten), history of groups, etc. At one point I ended up with Hebrew scholars, since the traditional religious service in order to consider the service valid is ten men above the age of 13 (bar mitzvah age). From there I ended up in Hassidism and the study of the kabbala, mysticism, and the theory of numbers in kabbala. My results were disappointing. I found no answers. Possibly the roots are to be found in anthropology, but that was my experience.

FREQUENCY OF GROUP MEETINGS AND COMBINED THERAPY

The members of the group meet with the group leader twice a week and some groups meet even more frequently. Some groups meet once a week and group members are seen individually once or twice a week; this is called combined therapy. While this practice is used by many group leaders, I have not found it particularly helpful. I find that the group members look forward to the individual therapy sessions and insufficient weight is given to the group experience. In short, the group experience becomes diluted. While there are some patients who may profit from combined therapy, specifically the acutely depressed and the acutely narcissistic who want and sometimes need considerable extra attention, it is my impression that those practitioners of combined therapy have a degree of reservation concerning a full commitment to the group method of treatment. It is as if the *real* problems can always be discussed in confidence with the benign and understanding therapist. I actively discourage individual visits with the group leader once a patient enters a group, unless there are exceptional circumstances where a patient feels completely unable to share feelings with the group. Recently, with the advent of co-therapy techniques as well as conjoint therapy, some group therapists have worked with patients who are in individual treatment with someone else. There are several rationales behind this approach, the major one being that it serves as a transition phase for patients who are very anxious about leaving individual treatment. This *seems* to be a good rationale but my experience has questioned the wisdom of this procedure. It's a case of the finest theory defeated by the ugly fact. What happens often in clinical practice is that the group members become resentful concerning the "outsider"—the individual therapist who knows about them but to whom they cannot relate. Perhaps there is envy involved—you are getting something that I'm not getting—but there is a good deal of anger involved. The practice has been used successfully by me on several occasions when there is (1) good and open contact with the individual therapist and (2) when the individual therapist has no neurotic need to hold onto the patient. A good clinical technique when one accepts such a patient for a group is to listen to the language of the referring therapist. A woman who was referred to me was described in every other sentence as "very beautiful." The clinical impression was that the individual therapist was very attracted to her. This was validated because while she was quite eager to leave treatment with him and use the group as the sole treatment modality he kept calling me and offering reasons as to why it was not a good idea.

DURATION OF MEETINGS

The group generally meets for one and one/half hours and is involved with the psychological needs of the patients who are group members. Sometimes a group may meet for a longer period of time, depending upon unusual circumstances. But unusual circumstances is not material that comes up at the end of a group session where the therapist is unable to bring the group meeting to an end. There are patients who because of resistance mechanisms will consistently wait until the last five or ten minutes of a group session before they bring up material. Actually, they trap both therapist and group members and use this as a mechanism to feel "short-changed" rather than explore resistances. Rather I mean "unusual circumstances" such as the sudden death of a group member or an unusual accident or suicide where group members express a need and desire for more time. This is NOT to be confused with a marathon approach to therapy which is not the focus of this chapter. Parenthetically, it may be stated that since resistance mechanisms are very subtle and complex there remain many questions as to what advantages are obtained by the confrontation techniques used in prolonged marathon therapies. The emphasis seems to be upon behavioral modification. Students have often asked me, "Why one and one/half hours?" The answer is that the time span is wearying for the therapist if it is truly a very interactional and intrapsychic group. Many years ago I conducted a survey of psychoanalysts as to their feelings about group psychoanalytic therapy. This was long before group therapy had gained its present prominence. One experienced psychoanalyst stated that he had used group approaches during World War II in the Dutch resistance army. He found the technique so complex and the material so profound that he gave up, feeling that it was impossible for a psychoanalyst to absorb and make sense of the enormous amount of data. He used the phrase "au dessus de la mélée," a phrase which captures the complexity of the group. Perhaps influenced by that phrase I find that an over-long group session, certainly one longer than two hours, generally seems to fatigue both group members and group leader. Perhaps my own sense of restlessness communicates itself to the group members, but I doubt this.

THE ALTERNATE MEETING

After the group has been meeting for some months the group leader should suggest that the group meet on its own without his being present. These meetings, called "alternate", "after group", or "extra group" sessions, are a natural outgrowth of the desire of the group members to maintain contact with one another. Some therapists are concerned that this leads to a kind of therapy subculture where group members use the group as a substitute for living. This is a real possibility as anyone who has witnessed Esalen or human potential movement can testify.

It seems more reasonable to make use of the desire of group members to maintain some post-group or out-of-formal-group-meeting contact. If the group leader sets up a climate where the work to be done is therapeutic, the group members will rapidly follow this lead. Occasionally in a newly formed group a group member will attempt to "seduce" the group by turning such a meeting into a drinking, eating or party type affair. This is to be discouraged, not by admonition, but by exploration of the dynamics at work. One group member who owned a restaurant would urge group members to meet at the restaurant after closing hours. It appeared to be a reasonable solution since the restaurant was centrally located. As in all restaurants, there is always food left after a busy day and it seemed wasteful to throw away such fine fare.

By the time the group members had stuffed themselves there was no appetite left to work at the problems that had brought them together. The restaurant owner was busy acting out her problem of the "good Jewish mother" who used food as a substitute for love and she acted this out against the background of her new family—the group. The group members, like all good children, found difficulty in rejecting their loving mother's cuisine, and the group leader had to step in rather forcefully. One of the best ways, if there is no spontaneous comment from a group member about the last scheduled meeting or the events after the meeting, is to ask if there are any feelings about the last meeting. This is an ice-breaker and is part of the "chain" of group sessions where the effort is to keep a continuity at work.

There is a major criticism of alternate or after group meetings which seems valid. There are some group leaders who prefer to keep the group meetings at a high level of anxiety. The rationale is that anxiety promotes change and therefore any meeting of group members other than the regularly scheduled meetings may serve to dissipate the level of anxiety. One group therapist actively prohibits group members from meeting outside of regularly scheduled sessions. He will discharge any group member from treatment who insists on extra-group contacts. Needless to say, he is a rather forceful individual who runs a "tight ship." While his rationale makes sense as he conceives of treatment, there is a question in my mind as to whether he is making maximum use of the desire of group members to meet outside of his purview. First, it would seem democratic to encourage group members to use their own resources without the group leader. Second, it may serve to encourage dependency if the group leader always has to be present. Third, some group members use extra-group sessions as a time to "rehearse" the kind of anger or irritation they may fear expressing in front of the group leader. As they become a little less frightened, or gain some measure of support from other group members, they gain enough confidence to confront the group leader. There is always the nagging possibility that the group leader, outside of his rationale (expressed), may have the anxiety that the group will "get out of hand" if he is not present, so he overcontrols. The major fear that students and colleagues have expressed concern "sexual acting out".

My answer is that patients have generally been involved in much acting out long before they came to treatment. If there is acting out, a rare experience in my practice, it should be explored and analyzed, since that is what treatment is all about. There are some disturbed therapists who encourage sexual acting out with a climate of social activity in their groups. These are the group leaders who promote birthday parties, Christmas parties, wedding celebrations, etc. Fortunately, these therapists appear to be in a minority. There is a question of trust in the patient that is at work when one discusses meetings without the group leader.

There is some question as to what is the best time in the new group's development to suggest that group members meet on their own. If the group has been meeting for some time the group members will after a regularly scheduled session encourage the new member to join them in an after group meeting or any other type of arrangement they may prefer, such as meeting on a different day. In the newly-formed group the leader will have to take the initiative. My clinical experience indicates that after the newly-formed group has had and survived its first explosion, ventilation of negative feelings, and the members have come together with the group leader present to explore and interpret, they are then ready to be encouraged to meet on their own. Otherwise there is a real risk that the explosion which has never occurred with the group leader present will occur in his absence and the group members will simply not return to treatment because of the anxiety over the aggression that has been brought to the surface.

Also, it does not seem prudent to provide a setting for members to meet without the group leader. It is like providing a home without the parent being present. Some group leaders state that because of "reality" problems such as inconvenience in finding a suitable meeting place they provide their own offices when they are not present. This seems to defeat the idea of group members meeting on their own. It also promotes a climate of "Big Daddy is always there." This is the very thing that the therapist should attempt to dispel with the statement that the group members meet on their own.

The group meetings without the group leader also serve as a

bridge for time intervals when the group leader is on vacation, or is ill, or for a variety of reasons is unable to be present with the group.

SELECTION OR SUITABILITY?

What has been described to this point about the group hopefully conveys some of my optimism in working with people in groups. This should convey some of the feelings at work when patients are approached with the idea of joining a group. As one gains in experience and maturity, the professional community may perceive the practitioner as a *group* person. When patients are referred with that idea in mind I rapidly move into the misconception. I point out that as a professional I reserve the right to use a variety of modalities to work with the patient. Sometimes the individual comes to treatment with the idea of joining a group. This person is often the worst candidate for a group and should be actively discouraged, since the group becomes a hiding place where a patient may be socially charming or overtly cooperative while in truth there is no effort made to work at depth therapy. Often the patient who comes for treatment experiences the idea of entry into the group, when first suggested by the psychoanalyst, as an enormous rejection. The patient may conceal the feeling that he is experiencing rejection and acquiesce to being placed in the group, but before too much time has passed this will manifest itself in a variety of responses. From absenteeism, ostensibly based on illness, to urgent business matters which preclude group attendance, the message is clear. The patient has NOT been adequately prepared for entry into the group. For this reason, I prefer to move slowly when discussing entry into the group. Sometimes patients will be scheduled before or after a group meeting. They may in the following individual session comment about the "large group of people in the waiting room." Or the patient may have heard from the referral source that I work with groups. Generally, in the first meeting with the newly referred patient I mention that I work with people both individually and in groups. I then drop the subject until some visits have passed where I will bring it up if the patient mentions it. It is only after some months have passed that I will, if I think it is indicated, bring up the idea of a group. Many group leaders move much more quickly toward placement of a patient in the group. I do not believe it is a good practice until a positive transference has been developed which is strong enough to sustain a patient who first confronts the intense movement in the group. When the patient first confronts the intra-psychic material at work there may be a tendency to run away. Based on a trust in the psychoanalyst, a trust which has been developed in individual visits, the patient will usually remain in the group if the analyst requests that the patient "sweat it out."

Somewhere in his writing Freud used the metaphor of the cooking pot made of clay that heats up quickly and cools off quickly. This would be in contrast to the pot that heats slowly and retains its heat over a period of time. This is in line with my thinking about the patient's progress in treatment as well as placement in the group. The patient who moves carefully and slowly shows a series of resistance mechanisms that should be approached and carefully analyzed will generally make more progress in treatment. The over-enthusiastic patient, for the most part, will become easily discouraged as both patient and therapist approach the difficult and painful parts of therapy. There is a type of patient who seems all gung-ho for group treatment and rapidly turns out to be a great asset for the group. This type of patient comes regularly, participates, assists the analyst, but never really gets to the problems that have brought him to treatment. After a while it becomes evident that the group is a substitute for living. This type of patient must be carefully evaluated before suggesting a group or going along with his enthusiasm.

The interaction in group therapy is verbal as opposed to recreational or other motor methods. This does not deny the importance of body posture, seating arrangements, facial mannerisms and other non-verbal communications. Because of the basic emphasis on verbal there may be a tendency on the part of the group therapist to be too eager to include a prospective patient who appears verbally fluent. Again, this is liable to be a major mistake. Often the subdued and thoughtful patient is a far greater asset to the group.

Although patients may appear ready to join a group there is often a great anxiety expressed just prior to entry into the group. This seems to be a general trend whether the patient is the supposedly sophisticated professional or the patient who is rather limited in formal cultural experiences. This is all part of resistance and should be analyzed. While the patient may need some encouragement and support at this time, the focus of the therapy should be upon the psychodynamics. The therapist, in his own eagerness, should not be misled. Inevitably the therapist may have made plans for the group composition and membership and he must be on guard so that his own planning doesn't overwhelm the patient's manifest as well as unexpressed anxiety.

The thrust of this chapter concerns groups of patients that are ambulatory, meet in a psychotherapist's office, come on their own, and leave on their own. The principles at work, with some modifications, are applicable to institutional settings as well as outpatient clinics. The therapist in private practice, for the most part, is probably far more selective in his or her own recruitment of patients. Indeed, one psychiatrist has speculated that as the psychotherapist becomes increasingly mature and "squared away" in his own psyche, he will find less and less need to work with disturbed patients, who theoretically can no longer be of help to the psychotherapist. As a result, the experienced psychotherapist raises his fees, becomes a supervisor, becomes an administrator or teacher, and in essence avoids contact with patients. All of this is done unconsciously by the therapist. It's a theory that may appeal to some people and is presented here in a rather cursory form for the reader to mull over.

But those of us who may still be working out our problems, according to the theory, how do we go about choosing patients for the group? One very motoric therapist had a need to choose patients who were lethargic or depressed. These were her favorites. It almost seemed as if she were defying her patients and challenging them so that they dare not remain neurotic. The rumor was that she would *will* patients to health. There are group therapists whose personality lends itself to particular types of patients with whom they are especially successful. While directing a department of a clinic some time ago I recall two group therapists who were particularly successful with specific groups. One suffered from problems of overweight and preferred to work with patients who had psychosomatic problems. She was very tuned in to their problems and very astute clinically. Another therapist was a rather removed and detached individual who seemed to be floating about in space most of the time. She worked very effectively with patients who were ambulatory psychotics or borderline psychotics, or those called pseudoneurotic schizophrenics. On those occasions where I would sit in with the group there was a complete fantasy quality to the group. Patients seemed to be lost in their own reveries and it appeared to be an inpatient mental hospital setting. Yet the rather detached group therapist would sit with the group, for what seemed to be long periods of time, while members rambled on and slowly, ever so slowly, group members seemed to improve. At least they were able to return to work and begin to play an active role in the society. The point is that the therapist's personality plays a large part in the selection process and this cannot be ignored.

Many group therapists have devoted much time to the question of selection of patients for the group. It would seem that they have become too enmeshed in psychiatric nomenclature. The very word selection finds its origins in the word choice, and further, discriminating choice. The object quality is perpetuated in the idea of selection and the idea works against the concepts of group therapy. It is possible that those group therapists who prefer to place patients in a group after very few individual sessions must prefer to stress very strong criteria against which they will work. It is not too unlike the more inexperienced therapist who relies heavily on psychometric evaluation to the exclusion of his own clinical judgment, which he does not feel too at ease with. (Also, many therapists who stress an intellective approach rely heavily on diagnostic criteria.) If the therapist has seen the patient for a longer period of time he will trust his own clinical judgment more and be less apt to rely upon selection per se. The more the novice reads about selection, the more confused he becomes since statements are often contradictory.

A preferable concept is the one of suitability. This stresses the idea of compatibility of a group of patients; how they will relate and interact with one another. This follows the concept of gestalt: the whole is larger than the sum of its parts. A group of patients becomes a therapy group and suddenly new forces are at work, changing configurations and different interpersonal forces at work in every meeting of the group and in every different group. Since I value the affective and human experience in group psychotherapy, I veer away from the doctrinaire and the specific and tend to take more risks. This, in turn, influences the question of which patients I will work with, since essentially I am optimistic about a patient's capacity for growth. An overemphasis on pathology seems to cast a pall over treatment. This is particularly seen in hospitals, where once the diagnosis is made a cloud seems to hang over treatment.

As was noted earlier, strong and very directive therapists appear to attract rather dependent patients. In institutional frameworks patients are often ordered to therapy groups and this places an additional burden upon the group leader who has to work with reluctant patients. With patients who are self-referred this is not a major problem, but the resistances that exist are quite deep-seated. The group leader should not impose a favorite project upon the group. One student, years ago, described to a class how he placed in a group a man whose particular problem led him to carry a live hand grenade with him to group meetings. But the therapist assured the class that the patient would be seated next to the group leader to preclude any acting out. The therapist seemed to ignore his own responsibility to the other members of the group. For example, the possibility of a coronary which he might experience was judged to be so vague a possibility that he believed that he could cope with all contingencies. This example is an extreme one, but is illustrative of the sort of cul-de-sac a therapist might work into. In another case, an experienced group therapist decided to place into an ongoing group a woman who was quite actively hallucinating. She would sit on the floor in the center of the group or roll about on the floor—this was many years before the encounter group movement. After some months, with the therapist being consistently over-protective of the woman, the group members exploded. They attacked her irrationality and the group therapist for burdening them. The therapist jumped to the woman's defense and she began to attack him verbally, stating that the group members were more authentic in their responses than his overprotectiveness. Only at that point did she begin to make some progress when the group members set limits. It should be clarified that in some group experiences patients have experienced a break with reaity. I have "sweated it out" within the group and the patients have worked out the psychotic episode within the group. But this is a patient who has been working with the group for some time.

Currently it is interesting that in many facilities there is a swing to the use of non-professional therapists. One of the major reasons advanced is that these therapists are not locked into a pattern of viewing patients in terms of psychiatric nomenclature. This seems to be along the lines of what has been noted to this point concerning suitability.

Selection has been defined in biology as a process that results or tends to result in the prevention of individuals or groups of organisms from surviving and propagating and at the same time allowing others to do so. Suitability, which is synonymous with compatibility, is defined as that which is suited to one's own needs, wishes or condition. If suitability is chosen as the method of operation, the initial interviews should be concerned with the patient's history of relatedness and a previous history of mutualism. Aristotle defined man as a social animal and in many years of experience I have only come across one patient who denied that definition. He was an extreme isolate and had experienced only minimal gratification in his early childhood relationships. This type of patient will require extensive individual therapy before he could even be considered for a group experience. There is also a category of patients who come from environments where they "wheel and deal" and constantly engage in power operations. This type of patient is usually very provocative and encourages anger, rejection and ultimately a paucity of group interaction. The group attempts to "freeze" this type of patient out of the group.

It seems almost impossible to set up standards for group suitability, but a patient is a candidate for a group in private practice or in an outpatient clinic if he:

a) has reality contact

b) can serve at times as a catalyst for the group

c) can be related to interpersonally

d) has sufficient flexibility so that he may reduce or heighten intragroup tensions.

A patient should not be placed in a group if he:

a) evokes reality-based fears in group members because he is impulse motivated, destructive and overtly anti-social

b) is in constant anxiety and the anxiety is of such acute nature that the group members feel overwhelmed and burdened

c) is so stimulated by his own unconscious feelings that his behavior is constantly chaotic as a result of which he cannot be reached by other members of the group

d) paralyzes interaction over an extended period of time.

To illustrate:

a) A patient worked as a policy numbers runner and carried a revolver. He was intensely anti-social and prone to violent rages. He was a poor candidate for the group.

b) A young woman, born in Germany, was extremely narcissistic. She was a refugee, but had escaped most of the Nazi terror. Her father, a physician, would saturate her with tranquilizers. Because of her rage and dependency and the additional physiological reality of her over-medication, each day was experienced by her as the end of the world. She fulfilled her father's needs and was the "complete patient." She was constantly in escapades and burdened the group members so that they were reduced to giving advice. She was removed from the group.

c) A woman wanted to enter the group. She was actively hallucinating and mumbling to herself and could not relate to other group members.

d) A married couple entered a group and spent much of the time in violent arguments. They showed little or no desire to explore beneath the anger. They should not have been in the same group.

Sometimes a therapist overlooks certain features in assessing patients. In one group a man was employed as a policeman and therefore was required to carry a revolver when he was not on official duty. One evening, at an alternate meeting of the group, he began to brandish a revolver at several group members. The group therapist was reached by a group member who managed to absent herself from the room in which the group was meeting. He went to the group and managed to disarm the policeman. In another one of my groups a landscape gardener would brandish a switchblade knife that he carried about in the greenhouses when he would want to make a cutting of plant stock. He evoked realistic fears and was removed from the group. He had used the experience as a way of interrupting his membership in the group.

On the other hand, a patient diagnosed as borderline schizophrenic was able to maintain reality contact. He moved slowly and was able to observe and relate to other group members. However, a severely psychotic patient who was being cared for at home could only relate in a group setting at a day hospital. The group was strongly leader led and the therapist was quite directive. In an outpatient group in private practice the anxiety level of the group would produce more and more psychotic material which the patient would be unable to cope with.

The acutely anxious patient looks mainly for relief of manifest anxiety. Essentially, he desires a supportive experience and is not interested in exploration of basic problems. He rarely works out well in a psychoanalytic group. Neither does the acutely depressed patient. A man came to treatment because his wife had left him and wanted to marry another man. His experience of rejection was so intense that he fell into an acute depression which masked his murderous impulses. The group members sensed the rage which the patient could not face. He preferred to obsess about his wife's infidelity. After a short time he became a great burden upon the group and began to halt group interaction.

There is a class of patient which I call *provocateurs*. They are generally very verbal and quite helpful at the outset of placement in a group. But their main strength seems to be their capacity to antagonize others. When patients lash back the provocateurs feel abused and misunderstood and retreat to individual therapy.

Very dependent patients who have never experienced much

affection in infancy need a long course of individual treatment with the therapist before entry into the group. Some group therapists see this type of patient in combined therapy. The stress in the groups that I organize is upon heterogeneity as in life; therefore, patients stem from difficult cultures, occupations, and have a variety of presenting problems. However, narcotic addicts and alcoholics are best grouped together. Their orality is so overwhelming, and their need for immediate gratification is so intense, that in the heterogeneous group other group members experience these patients as an especially heavy burden. The group experience for these patients is largely educational, where they learn something about social relationships. One therapist who works primarily with members of the clergy, found that they were much more receptive to inclusion of very demanding patients in the same group. Apparently their theological training prepared them for helping others. On the other hand, this may be the very problem which should be worked out and which may be masked.

Active psychopaths excite the group, interest group members with tales of derring do, but in reality contribute little or nothing. They are best excluded. After group members have listened with fascination to tales of robbery, procuring, etc. there is no evidence that intrapsychic material is exposed or dealt with. Generally, this type of patient may be referred by a court to therapy as part of a sentence. These individuals are not too different from patients who blunder into treatment which is depth-oriented and who desire relief from pressing current problems. The effort is to gain a speedy solution for an immediate problem and there is no desire to gain insight.

Patients who are suffering from incurable illness can profit from specially organized groups which will help them cope with dying, but the ongoing group will feel frustrated and helpless with the dying patient and an air of pessimism will rapidly develop. If a group member develops an incurable disease while in treatment the patient is permitted to remain. The group is generally supportive and it may serve as a stimulus for other patients to live life more fully. Suicidal patients can be included in a group since their very presence and willingness to enter a group offers some hope. Generally, the enormous rage that is underneath the despair can be handled by other group members. There are patients who are dramatic and constantly threaten suicide. But even here threats should not be ignored.

I have had very poor experiences with overtly sado-masochistic patients. The pattern of suffering promotes concern from other group members. They finally realize that they have been trapped and begin to lash out. This, in turn, satisfies the need of the patient to be punished and as a result the group grinds to a halt. Session after session is taken up with these maneuvers. One patient, Anne, became sexually involved with a man in the group. He would meet with her after the group sessions and she would go with him to a deserted part of the city where she would practice fellatio while they were sitting in his auto. He would then urinate in her mouth and over her body while she expressed cries of joy. The two patients refused for a long time to discuss their acting out and after much inquiry on the part of the therapist Anne complained that she was being "tortured" by the questions which "disrupted her romance." The group was very angered and both patients finally had to leave the group. The man, Irving, a psychopath, once came to the group and stated that he was so grateful to the therapist that he had purchased a gift for him, a shirt. While it is against my policy to accept gifts, the patient protested so strongly that I decided to accept the gift. After several sessions Irving stated that he had stolen the shirt from the store where he was employed as a salesman. He seemed very gleeful as he described how he had "tricked" the group leader.

While some group therapists would discourage the "habitual monopolist" from entering the group, this has not been my experience. Apparently concern is expressed that the monopolist will dominate the group by compulsive talking. Finally, the group is supposed to become very frustrated. However, if the therapist has developed a strong relationship with this type of patient, he may be able to place him in a group and point out that it would be to his interest to remain silent for some period of time rather than mask his intense insecurity by compulsive verbalization.

There has been some debate in the literature concerning the suitability of overt homosexuals in the heterogeneous group. This should not present any difficulty with a relatively sophisticated group. I do not believe in the concept of the adjusted homosexual and prefer to deal with the symptom as I would deal with any other symptom—including that of the compulsive heterosexual man who has the need to seduce women, or the promiscuous woman who must seduce men, for both of these kinds of patients are often quite homosexual if there is any depth exploration.

Previously, the depressed patient has been discussed. There are depressed patients who present a picture of limited intellect. They are not retarded, but are emotionally blocked. Careful psychological testing will be of help so that the therapist is able to differentiate between limited intelligence and emotions which block an individual's intellectual functioning.

The therapist as he gains in clinical and life experience will become less reliant on rigid classification and more trusting of his own intuitiveness. He will trust the patient's capacities more and work with the patient's uniqueness. He will then be more at ease with the concept of suitability.

Through all of the therapist's contact with the patient he should always be aiming toward the group, if this is his belief. Therefore, through this period he will develop a pool of patients who will be available as replacements. He should be concentrating on the transference and the establishment of a positive transference that will promote ease of movement into the group. He should be concentrating on the patient's resistances. The majority of patients have been failed by their original group—the family. The idea of entering a new family—the therapy group—and coming to grips with the problems that have been buried so unsuccessfully fills the patient with much ambivalence of feeling. Every patient wants to change and yet wants to stay neurotic. Shakespeare phrased it well: "Better the devil we know than the devil we know not." With all the patient's ostensible agreement with the therapist's plan, there may be a total masking of the patient's real fear and anxiety about being rejected by the therapist once the patient is in the group. This is a good time for the therapist to spend time—extra time—in looking for any indications in the dream or fantasy material that shed some light on the patient's feelings about imminent entry into the group.

The dream and fantasy material change quite dramatically once the patient is really aware that the group experience will happen very soon. If the preparation is carefully worked out for each patient there is little risk of rejection. But sometimes patients have had unsuccessful individual treatment and have been experiencing feelings of hopelessness. They view referral to a group therapist as entry into second-rate psychotherapy. If this is not clarified very quickly the group experience is poor for both patient and novice group therapist. This is especially bad if two or three of such patients enter the same group. Little group interaction will occur and everyone in the group ends up quite discouraged.

The novice therapist in work with groups may find himself pushing a patient toward the group. This is always a poor idea for it helps the patient bury his resistances and defeats the psychoanalytic process. While the establishment of the positive transference has been stressed, it should not be misused. The patient should be given the opportunity to express resistances and indeed urged to express and confront anxieties about group membership. There are occasions when a therapist despairs of working with a patient and uses the group as a last resort. This is a time where the therapist uses the group to mask his own intrapsychic problems and the group is used punitively. While the patient may not express his resentment he will enter the group reluctantly and really on the way out. Careful preparation cannot be stressed too much. While there are therapists who are so eager about group treatment that they "enthuse" patients about the value of the group, this is not unlike a "hard sell campaign." In such a case the treatment is repressive and constructive and transference phenomena are ignored. There are therapists who cannot work with patients individually and are, therefore, eager to praise group treatment as a complete answer to all of life's problems. They are misguided. So, too, are those therapists who cannot bear to share patients with the group. The patient who is carefully prepared for the group will expose his deep-seated anxieties about what group therapy means to him.

CO-THERAPY

Many novice group therapists have learned about group therapy as co-leaders of a group. This is unfortunate because they have never learned to lead a group without another therapist present. This situation exists in many hospitals and clinics. It serves as a training experience for psychiatrists in training, as well as psychologists, social workers and nurses. This often proves to be a very satisfactory solution for the staffing problems of a clinic or hospital but it doesn't make sense for the complete training of a psychotherapist. For it is only when the therapist is confronted with the sole responsibility of group leadership, without any feeling that there is someone there to "bail him out" that he can truly feel the awesome burden of functioning as a group leader. Some clinics and hospitals encourage visitors to therapy groups. This is a bad idea. It is disruptive and feeds the patient's fantasies that he is an object of clinical scrutiny. If there must be someone present other than the group leader, that person should be either a recorder, participant observer or trainee.

The presence of a co-therapist often increases interaction and enlarges the group process. The patient, while questioning one interpretation, may be more responsive to the same interpretations from two therapists who are leading the group. Even differences in interpretation between therapists can be accepted by the patients if there is a healthy mutualism at work so that the therapists genuinely respect one another. Of course, the presence of two therapists modifies the transference responses, but this is all "grist for the mill," and should be analyzed. Co-therapy in the psychoanalytic group often breaks through blockages. Indeed, when there is a complete standstill in the individual psychoanalysis, the presence of another therapist may provoke a breakthrough. The presence of a co-therapist in the group often works at the task of undercutting patient's defenses. A patient may find it intolerable if the group therapist he relates to undercuts long term defenses. However, if the patient feels that he can fall back upon the co-therapist who is not working at the defense mechanisms, he will not feel so deserted or threatened. In groups where there is a good deal of intrapsychic disturbance the presence of a co-therapist helps the other therapist maintain psychic balance while the world of the unconscious is entered. Sometimes the material is so overwhelming that even the group therapist has a difficult time maintaining contact with reality.

It is important that the novice group therapist, or even the experienced therapist have a theoretic rationale before attempting co-therapy with a group. Many group leaders have seized upon a technique because it sounds "like a good idea." But there are very real problems when two therapists decide to work with one another. Very often there is rivalry at work between co-therapists. Or the trainee sits in a group while the experienced therapist runs the group. If the group is conceptualized like the original family, a working hypothesis which seems as reasonable as any other, it may indeed confuse patients who observe co-therapists, one leading and the other following. It may re-awaken the original family and the anxiety about the family, as well as the anger toward the dominating parent and the irritation felt toward the passive and submissive parent. This is all to the good if the co-therapists work with the transference responses. Generally, novice therapists ignore or are unaware of the forces at work and ignore the sexual transferences at work. Generally, transferences are ignored when co-therapists have not carefully defined why they are working together. In hospitals and clinics co-therapists are often thrown together with little regard for the needs of the therapists or patients and too much attention given to the staffing of the hospital or clinic. This is a poor arrangement which is destructive to both patients and staff. There should be attention paid to the compatibility of both therapists, specifically their ability to be comfortable with differences and respect for one another's style of work. When there is no mutual regard at work one therapist may be provoked by a sudden interpretation offered by his co-therapist which he does not understand. Or the rivalry which has not been explored may manifest itself in a competition for the patient's affection or attention. The patient may respond to this and like the child encourage the parents, in the guise of the therapists, to compete with one another.

Group therapists in private practice often decide to join as co-therapists based on friendship of some duration. But what makes for a good friendship does not necessarily make for good co-therapy. The type of openness and authenticity needed in co-therapy may not be at work in the friendship. This is not to deny friendship between co-therapists, but merely to question it as a selection factor.

Some group therapists are attuned to the idea of a male therapist and a female therapist working together as they lead a group. The theory behind this is to activate the transference responses to the father and mother. Similarly, the male and female may serve as models for the group. The weakness behind this rationale is related to the problem of ascertaining whether the male therapist is male and whether the female is not in fact quite masculine. Rather than serving as a model, the co-therapists may further confuse the patients, particularly if they avoid the basic problems that exist between them.

There are instances when novice group therapists work with more experienced therapists and the effort is made to confront the senior therapist. Or the novice may be fearful of challenging the senior therapist's interpretations even when they are obviously in error. Ideally, co-therapists should be able to supplement one another. They should accept and respect one another and have a commonality of goals in treatment of the group. They should not be competitive, defensive or engage in activities which are calculated to undermine one another. All of this should be clarified before both therapists meet with the group and, while problems will come up when they begin to work with one another, it is far better to have these major differences resolved before work begins with the group.

It is a good idea in any type of clinical situation that both therapists interview potential group members together. The patient is then prepared from the beginning for the idea of a co-therapy group. This is the ideal situation but it is in line with the effort to work at transference responses from the outset of treatment. While many therapists avoid the problem, it is important that a fee policy be established as well as a clear understanding be arrived at as to how fees are to be collected and shared. This avoids the possibility of one therapist taking on active responsibility while the other remains passive and plays the role of the "nice guy."

FEES AND THE PAYMENT OF THE THERAPIST

Whether a group is led by co-therapists or by one therapist, the fee problem is critical in treatment. The patient, suffering from minimal feelings of worth, will generally feel that his only importance to the therapist is based upon the fee that is paid. While the therapist wants to be reimbursed for his services, he should make it clear that his time is being hired and not his interest and concern. This should be established at the outset of treatment. The group therapist should be very clear as to his fee structure and his own sense of self-worth. Many therapists are not too sure what they are worth and attempt to avoid the dynamic implications of the fee by many circuitous and neurotic mechanisms. They may mail out bills, delay in collecting fees, or assign the task of collecting fees to a secretary or receptionist. This last situation often occurs in a clinic. This is all very unfortunate because much of the dynamic material is obscured. The novice therapist is better off charging all of the patients the same fee. When he is more comfortable with his skills he may consider different fee structures for various members of the group. At the outset of his own group leadership he may find it intolerable to face the rage that patients express when they find out that different members of the group are paying more or less. Any problems with fees should be discussed in the group since the fee is part of dynamics and patients should be encouraged to discuss their feelings about fees and what this represents for them. In my experience, the payment of the fee by the patient directly to the therapist makes the therapy more meaningful and personal. It takes therapy to the authentic base. Some therapists with a mail billing approach maintain the aura of the benign father or mother and the fee is never discussed; it simply is masked in the magic of the post office mailing. A bill goes out, a check is received, and money is never considered an ingredient of treatment. The way in which the patient pays or doesn't pay is ignored or never analyzed. This is a loss to all concerned. For most working class patients it is preferable to bill them weekly and insist on a weekly payment, otherwise a large debt accumulates which may be overwhelming to the patient.

THE SETTING OF THE GROUP

Group psychoanalytic therapy has been practiced in a variety of different settings. The physical locale should be conducive to intrapsychic and interpersonal exploration. If a telephone is present it should be muted and preferably not answered during the group session. It is a rare and gifted therapist who can interrupt the complexities of the group process, answer the phone and then get back to the group. The rooms should be comfortable, adequate ventilation should be provided. Some group leaders provide a separate room for the group sessions. As the group members interact they will sweat and give off much body heat and the room can become uncomfortable. The chairs should be comfortable and a good deal of thought should be given to this problem since the patients should be physically comfortable. When some chairs are seen as more desirable than others patients often invest much meaning in a chair—thus the group therapist's chair, if he always takes the same one, is seen as a very special chair. It is advisable that the therapist not take the same chair but shift from session to session. This is to preclude any static design. It is not important if patients prefer sitting on the floor; most do not, since the session is long and can be fatiguing. It is not advisable to have any barriers between members so a table in the center is *not* advisable. Over the years I have actively been opposed to cigarette or cigar or pipe smoking. I simply do not provide ash trays and explain that since I am working with psychical balance the support of smoking seems contradictory. Some patients bring their own ash trays and through the years there is less and less smoking. Eating, drinking, etc. is discouraged, since the effort is to preclude a party atmosphere. Sometimes group members that meet at noon or at a time period that invades the patient's lunch break bring sandwiches or a beverage. This is neither encouraged or discouraged. It has been observed that when patients become upset they have difficulty eating food that is brought to the group. Sometimes there is a special occasion—a birth, wedding or someone leaving the group—"graduating"—and members may bring some food or a beverage. This is acceptable and again neither discouraged or encouraged.

THE PRESENT AND THE FUTURE

Over the past twenty years there has been a subtle turn around in the approach to patients. There has been a shift from an over-preoccupation with what's wrong with the patient to a stress on what's right with the patient. For many years I have stressed the *person* quality of the individual who comes to treatment. The danger of the word *patient* is that there is a great concern for pathology and an unwillingness to tap the resources of the person who is in treatment. Currently, with the human potential movement, there is an idealization of the person's capacities and a tendency to minimize the neurotic and self-destructive mechanisms that are at work. While it is unfair to label suspicious people as paranoid, it is naive to ignore the malevolence at work in the acutely disturbed individual who has been classified as paranoid. The current battle in psychiatric circles concerns the dismantling of the massive mental hospitals where thousands of patients are lodged. This massing of human beings is alone enough to provoke psychotic reactions. There is the danger that the group approach will be used as the panacea for all of man's problems. There are psychoanalysts who use the group approach who become defensive and tend to become involved with fads in a desperate effort to be part of the tide. But the ethical practitioner should be both democratic and "elitist." For while he believes in the capacity of people he practices a complex technique which will require thoughtfulness. Technique is not the answer. Nor are simplistic answers.

The psychoanalytic approach to groups will demand much training and responsibility on the part of the group leader. This will present problems because he will often feel the desire to use simplistic approaches which obscure transference phenomena and ultimately obscure the intrapsychic and interpersonal forces at work. The big push in the 1970s is toward a behavioristic approach. It is questionable as to whether this approach can be reconciled with psychoanalytic concepts. There is no substitute for thorough training and a theoretic rationale in the practice of group therapy. Ultimately the rewards of professional competence justify the use of the intensive method called psychoanalytic group psychotherapy.

Suggested additional readings

Bach, G. (1954): *Intensive Group Psychotherapy*. New York: Ronald Press.

Foulkes, S. H. (1965): *Therapeutic Group Analysis*. New York: International Universities Press.

Golembiewski, R. T. and Blumberg, A. (Eds.) (1970): *Sensitivity Training and the Laboratory Approach*. Itasca, Illinois: Peacock Publishers.

Kaplan, H. I. and Saddock, B. J. (Eds.) (1971): *Comprehensive Group Psychotherapy*. Baltimore: Williams & Wilkins,

Mullan, H. and Rosenbaum, M. (1962): *Group Psychotherapy: Theory and Practice*. New York: Free Press.

Powdermaker, F. and Frank, J. D. (1953): *Group Psychotherapy*. Cambridge: Harvard University Press.

Rosenbaum, M. (1972): Group psychotherapy with adolescents. Chapt. 32 in *Manual of Child Psychopathology*. New York: McGraw-Hill.

Rosenbaum, M. and Berger, M. M. (Eds.) (1974): *Group Psychotherapy and Group Function*. New York: Basic Books (revised edition).

Slavson, S. R. (1964): *A Textbook in Analytic Group Psychotherapy*. New York: International Universities Press.

Whitaker, D. S. and Lieberman, M. A. (1964): *Psychotherapy Through The Group Process*. New York: Atherton Press.

Wolf, A. and Schwartz, E. K. (1962): *Psychoanalysis in Groups*. New York: Grune and Stratton.

Yalom, I. (1970): *The Theory and Practice of Group Psychotherapy*. New York: Basic Books.

Zuk, G. H. (1971): Family therapy: *A Triadic-Based Approach*. New York: Behavioral Publications.

Cooperating editor's note

DR. DOROTHY STOCK WHITAKER is author, with M. A. Lieberman, of *Psychotherapy Through the Group Process*, the clearest exposition of a "group-centered" approach which I have ever read. Those theoretical approaches which can be considered group centered include Bion and Eriel, English clinicians. The group centered approaches have had their most profound influence on the theory and functioning of British and South American group therapists. In the United States, there was profound resistance to the group centered approaches in the 1950's .Some therapists believe the individual was lost in the focus on group processes. Now in the early 1970's in the U.S. there is more acceptance of the importance of group level factors, with less fear that the individual will be lost.

What is the essence of the group centered approaches? The basic assumption is that it is *essential* to understand the group processes in order to understand the individual within the group. This leads to the therapist's double focus: one on the group-level processes and the other on the individual, especially in reaction to what's going on within the group. Another important assumption of the group centered approach is that successive comments made by different group members are similar to free associations of one patient in individual psychoanalysis. Understanding the group flow of free associations will help one move from the manifest content to the latent meanings of shared issues, which initially are usually unconscious.

Whitaker and Lieberman have brilliantly integrated these group-centered assumptions with ideas derived from Thomas French's focal conflict theory. In this paper on the formative phase of therapy groups, Whitaker's clinical statements clearly flow from their systematically developed theory.

A group centred approach

DOROTHY STOCK WHITAKER

THE CONCEPTUAL FRAMEWORK known as Group Focal Conflict Theory had its beginnings in 1955 or 1956, in a series of seminars conducted at the Veterans' Administration Research Hospital in Chicago. Dr. Thomas M. French, of the Chicago Institute for Psychoanalysis, was a consultant to the Psychiatric Service at that time. He had already developed his ideas about the nuclear and focal conflict and had demonstrated through careful clinical work the usefulness of these concepts for organising the diverse material of the psychoanalytic session, the dream, and indeed the personality itself. (French, 1952) During the same period, a small group of colleagues at the hospital had been working with and thinking about therapy groups, and had been struck by the fact that one could frequently identify shared themes in the group. That is, it appeared that the patients in a therapy group might work on some particular issue for a period of time—for example, the hazards of expressing resentment toward parents—then shift to some other theme having to do perhaps, with loneliness or feelings of having been deprived, return at some point to the issue of resentment towards parents, usually dealing with it in a rather different way and extending it, before again shifting to some other issue. These issues or themes were not merely a matter of content, but involved feelings, attitudes and positions vis-a-vis the theme: hopes, fears, worries, impulses, and wishes. Although particular patients did not participate in or react to the theme in exactly the same way, nevertheless one could see that as the interaction proceeded, something like a shared theme built up, prevailed for a while, and then shifted or dissolved. One could in in fact say that for a certain period of time something was 'focal' in the group.

It occurred to us that it might be interesting to test out the applicability of Dr. French's ideas to a group, and this was undertaken in a series of seminars. It soon became apparent that certain of the basic ideas in French's theory could be applied, but also that some modification and extension was required. A group, after all, is not a person. In no sense can it be regarded as a single organism and it does not have a history, or at least not one which is comparable to that of a person. Nevertheless we found as we rather laboriously went over tapes and protocols of group sessions that the shared themes already observed could be stated in group focal conflict terms. That is, they could be seen to involve a disturbing motive (shared wish) which was in conflict with a reactive motive (shared fear). In the terms of the theory, these two elements constitute a group focal conflict. One could also observe efforts on the part of the patients to cope with the shared conflict (wish vs. fear) by attempting to establish solutions. A solution was a way of dealing with the conflict which would above all reduce the level of anxiety in the group (the reactive motive). Sometimes a solution also allowed for some expression of the associated wish or impulse; sometimes it did not. In other words, the solutions which the patients constructed were primarily directed toward alleviating reactive fears but they also allowed for varying degrees of satisfaction of the disturbing motive or wish. In detail, all this worked out in ways which were different from that which could occur for the individual. For example, since a group does not have a history in the same sense as does an individual, it was not possible to identify a nuclear conflict to which later focal conflicts were reasonant. The concept of *nuclear* conflict, important in French's original formulation, thus does not appear in group focal conflict theory. Some aspects of French's original theory were relevant but took on a different form when applied to a group. For example solutions, being a product of a *group*, involve implicit collaboration or collusion among group members, and sometimes though not always involve role differentiation.

A first statement of theory appeared in the article, "The Group Focal Conflict" (Whitman and Stock, 1958), and in the next several years various aspects and application of this conceptual framework were discussed in further articles. These included "The deviant member in therapy groups" (Stock, Whitman and Lieberman, 1958); "The relation between individual and group conflicts in psychotherapy" (Whitman, Lieberman and Stock, 1960); and "Interpersonal concerns during the early sessions of therapy groups" (Stock, 1962). A comprehensively worked out statement of this conceptual framework appears in the book "Psychotherapy through Group Process" (Whitaker and Lieberman, 1964). In this book the conceptual framework is presented formally in a series of propositions pertaining to the development of the group, the experience of the individual, the group therapeutic process, and the management and exploitation of the group situation for the benefit of the individual.

In this series of publications we have, from time to time, devoted specific attention to early sessions. In the article published in 1962, typical shared wishes and fears which were found to emerge during early sessions were discussed, as well as typical solutions. Certain of the propositions presented in "Psychotherapy through the Group Process" have to do with the character of the formative phase of the group and a discussion is included of the kinds of interventions which a therapist may introduce to influence this formative phase toward a maximally useful therapeutic milieu.

In recent years I have conducted a number of seminars about group therapy with social workers, psychologists and psychiatrists. Seminar members have presented problem situations arising in a variety of settings, in some cases with populations not ordinarily regarded as psychiatric patients (e.g. prisoners, probationers, addicts, inadequate mothers). In these seminar discussions, the composition of the therapeutic group frequently emerges as important in setting the character of the early sessions. Sometimes, composition critically influences the ultimate success or failure of the group. It also has become clear that certain stresses on the therapist are particularly acute during the early sessions. In attempting to cope with these stresses, a therapist may find himself inadvertently colluding with the group to support certain shared defenses or undesirable interactive patterns.

This article pulls together, from earlier writings and subsequent experience, a statement about the formative phase of therapy groups. It includes a discussion of the character of early sessions, goals for the formative phase, the relevance of group composition, the therapist's task and tactics, and special stresses on the therapist.

A brief quotation from the book "Psychotherapy through the Group Process" will serve to summarize the group focal conflict point of view:

> The events of a group therapy session are conceptualised in terms of a slowly emerging, shared covert conflict consisting of two elements—a disturbing motive (a wish) and a reactive motive (a fear). These two elements constitute the group focal conflict. The term 'group focal conflict' summarises the key features of this view of groups, indicating that the disturbing and reactive motives conflict, pervade the group as a whole, and are core issues engaging the energies of the patients. Concommitant with the group focal conflict, one sees various attempts to find a solution. A group solution represents a compromise between the opposing forces; it is primarily directed to alleviating reactive fears but also attempts to maximise gratification of the disturbing motive. (Whitaker and Lieberman, 1964, p. 17).

It should perhaps be added that the group focal conflict and solution are both generated by and revealed by the successive comments made during the group session. The comments which follow one after another can be thought of as a sequence of associations made by different persons which accumulate to express a theme. Often, the most visible thing about a group is not the group focal conflict as such, which tends to be underlying and covert, but the solution, which tends to be expressed more directly in interaction or content. For example, if a group spends a great deal of time discussing some trivial topic, group focal conflict theory suggests that one think of this as a solution to some underlying shared conflict. The solution consists of collusive avoidance of something else. What the 'something else' is must be gleaned from hints derived from content, intonation, sequence of associations including interruptions and silences, and non-verbal behaviour. Developing hypotheses about the nature of the group focal conflict and related solutions is in itself a complex skill. (See the article "Methodological issues in the assessment of total-group phenomena in group therapy," Stock and Lieberman, 1962).

When solutions are examined it can be seen that they bear varying relationships to the associated group focal conflict. A distinction can be made between "enabling" solutions and "restrictive" solutions. Enabling solutions are those which alleviate reactive fears and at the same time allow for the expression, recognition and exploration of the disturbing motive or wish. Thus enabling solutions are enabling in the further sense of allowing for open exploration of the feelings involved in the associated group focal conflict. They are liberating in character. Restrictive solutions are those which alleviate fears, but at the expense of allowing any sort of recognition or exploration of the associated disturbing motive. Thus they are restrictive in the further sense of precluding facing or exploring the impulses or wishes involved in the group focal conflict. Enabling and restrictive solutions of course lie on a continuum and many group solutions alleviate the fear whilst at the same time allowing for partial exploration of the associated wish. It should be borne in mind that all solutions, whether enabling or restricting, are functional for the group members, for they bind and alleviate shared fears and concerns.

In the beginning, one can expect a therapy group to establish primarily restrictive solutions. This is understandable if one keeps in mind the fact that a therapy group is an intrinsically threatening situation for most persons. In a group, members are aware that they are expected to discuss their problems and private concerns. This means discussing feelings and experiences of which they may be ashamed and which they may expect will elicit rejection and criticism from others. Further, they are expected to reveal these matters in the presence of unknown strangers, whose reactions cannot be predicted or relied upon. An individual could, of course, easily avoid these fears by never talking about himself at all. Some patients, and indeed some groups, invoke this solution temporarily. But patients are not only fearful of the group but also hope to benefit from it. This hope tends to push them toward wishing to express themselves despite their fears. It is this situation which sets the stage for the earliest group focal conflicts and solutions. The initial group focal conflict is likely to involve a disturbing motive having to do with some wish to express or share feelings and experiences, and a reactive motive having to do with some fear of the consequences of doing so. The feared consequences may be one of many: a fear of being shamed, ridiculed, or criticized by other patients; a fear of being shamed, ridiculed, or criticized by the therapist; a fear of being rejected, abandonned or expelled from the group by the therapist; a fear of being overwhelmed by one's own feelings or of being unable to cope with the material that one might oneself reveal; a fear of being made sicker than one aleady is by being exposed to the worries and concerns of other patients; and many specific variations of these. It is no wonder, then, that the first shared solutions one sees in a therapy group are likely to be restrictive in character. It is experienced as important above all to make the group a safe place. For a time at least the hopes of personal benefit may recede and the patients wish only to survive. Thus, during the early sessions one sees shared solutions which have the character of collusive defenses. The patients may talk about some trivial issue such as last night's television programme or the current football game; they may talk about the problems of some absent person (such as someone else on the ward or someone's relative or acquaintance); they may talk about some problem such as inferiority or loneliness in an abstract or intellectual way; they may encourage one of their members, less fearful or more exhibitionistic than the rest, to dominate the situation with his problems; they may cast one person into the role of "patient" and then question and "help" him; they may press the therapist to direct and structure the group, so that anything that is said is *his* responsibility; they may provide minimal information about themselves and then demand that the therapist provide advice or interpretations; and so on. Such solutions are not likely to be very therapeutically useful, but they function very well in allaying initial fears.

In speaking this way about the formative phase of a therapy group, one is perhaps in some danger of conveying an over-simplified picture of actual events. Observations of groups support the view that restrictive solutions tend to dominate the formative stage, and that enabling solutions are more characteristic of later stages and can then be maintained for longer periods. However, it is not the case that periods of useful discussion in the context of enabling solutions never occur during early sessions. Nor is it true that restrictive solutions are finished once and for all, never to reappear once the group is past its initial sessions. Even the use of the term "formative phase" is misleading if one takes it to mean that something uniquely different appears during early sessions, or that a particular moment in time occurs when a group can be clearly said to have completed its formative phase and to have moved on to something quite different. In reality, a group moves in fits and starts; it progresses, regresses, gets stuck and extricates itself. It makes sense to talk of a formative phase because in most groups a time arrives, usually within the first six or eight to ten or twelve sessions, when most of the early concerns have been explored at least once, and fears have been sufficiently reduced so that the patients do not need to cling quite so tenaciously or consistently to the initially-invoked restrictive solutions. The therapist tends to experience this subjectively as a sense of relief; he feels that the group will "go" and that some good will come of it.

Neither in practice nor in theory does one expect any group to operate indefinitely and consistently on enabling solutions even when it is well established. In fact, there are good reasons to expect that this is impossible in a well-functioning group. One expects a particular enabling solution to allow the group to explore the issue to which the solution pertains for a certain period of time. However, the very process of exploring is likely to lead the patients to new fears and concerns. These new fears and concerns tend to generate a new group focal conflict which might temporarily require a restrictive solution. If the group is continually working on its own frontiers then one would expect alternating episodes of enabling and restrictive solutions. One sees a kind of spiralling effect in which the group comes back to the same themes time after time, exploring them in a different way within somewhat wider boundaries.

Thinking specifically now of the formative phase, it is possible to state one's goals for the group both in general terms and in the terms of group focal conflict therory. What does the therapist hope the group will be like after the first six to eight sessions? Conversely, what does he hope the group will *not* be like? Most therapists, whatever their theoretical persuasion, hope that after the first few sessions of the group, the patients will feel reasonably at ease and mutually trusting, so that feelings and experiences ordinarily censored can be expressed and explored freely and openly in the group. Most therapists hope that after the first few sessions of the group the patients will *not* be mutually mistrustful, will not be careful about what can be expressed, will not operate within such narrow boundaries that many affects and experiences are censored out of the arena of the group. In group focal conflict terms, the therapist hopes that the group will soon come to operate primarily on enabling rather than restrictive solutions. He hopes that restrictive solutions, if they occur, will be transient phenomena and not become an established way of life for the group.

This statement of goals defines a task for the therapist and for the group. It suggests that the therapist will wish to do what he can during the formative stage of the group to help the group move toward predominantly enabling solutions and to avoid persistent reliance on restrictive solutions.

In considering what a therapist can do or need do to facilitate this movement, three points require discussion. First, is movement from predominantly restrictive to predominantly enabling solutions ever a spontaneous one, and can it therefore occur without specific attention from the therapist? Second, can the composition of the group either facilitate or forstall this movement? Third, what can the therapist do or say during the group sessions to facilitate this movement?

First, then, does a group ever move in this direction spontaneously? Very occasionally, this may occur. When it does, it is because the composition of the group is such as to facilitate this movement, and because the therapist does not interfere with it. A facilitating composition is one in which there is someone who is a bit less fearful than the others, and who can help the group test and resolve its fears around (let us say) intimacy, someone who is a bit less fearful than the others and who can help the group test and resolve its fears around hostility, etc. There is someone who is not satisfied to continue indefinitely with some restrictive solution, or someone who is not prepared to cooperate with some restrictive solution and thus prevents its permanent establishment. As might be expected, such ideally facilitative compositions are rare. More typically and more often, the group composition is not ideal and the therapist must expect to play some role in monitoring this aspect of the group situation and attempting to influence it.

(For the sake of completeness, one needs to point out that for spontaneous optimum development one needs not only a facilitating group composition but a therapist who does not obstruct the natural development of the group. The ways in which a therapist can spoil a group will be taken up later, following the discussion of tactics of intervention.)

Some compositions are inherently more difficult than others and more likely to lead to restrictive solutions becoming established as a stubborn and intractable way of life. At the extreme, certain group compositions simply will not work and cannot be influenced. Not long ago a student described an unsatisfactory group composed of middle-aged paranoid women who had been in a mental institution for a minimum of ten years. The group was described as silent and mutually mistrustful. The therapist found that he was driven to question and prod the group in order to get any participation at all. Any comment on the part of a patient elicited little or no response from others, and each comment that the therapist was able to dredge up was followed by a further period of suspicious silence. One could in fact expect little else of such a composition, since the individual tendencies of each member led her to maintain a distrustful silence whilst warily waiting for someone else to take risks. Since everyone in the group was like this, there was no-one who could be expected to break the pattern. In another group composed of young male obsessive-compulsives, the intellectualizing tendencies of each patient were supported and reinforced by similar predilections in all the other members of the group, and it proved impossible to move the group from a collusive defence of intellectualisation. In both instances the composition was at fault, for the homogeneity of the group with respect to preferred defences or preferred and habitual modes of interaction, were mutually reinforced and instantaneously translated into a shared way of life. No therapist is powerful enough to break through and influence this kind of massively maintained defence. This is not, of course, to say that one should never work with chronic paranoid patients or with young obsessive compulsives. It is to say, however, that groups homogeneously composed of such persons can be expected to be very difficult if not doomed to failure. What one wishes for, instead, is a varied composition in which heterogeneity exists with regard to preferred defence, preferred mode of interaction, and preferred affective expression. In such a group the intellectualisation of one will be counteracted by the impulsivity of another; the suspiciousness of one will fail to be supported by others. No single mode of defence has the opportunity to become established as a shared solution or norm. In "Psychotherapy through the Group Process," criteria for composing groups are discussed in some detail. It is pointed out that along with heterogeneity in preferred defence or mode of affective expression, homogeneity with regard to "level of vulnerability" is also desirable. The latter variable has to do with how quickly the individual is prepared to move, how soon he becomes threatened by the movement of the group and how resilient he is under stress. If the group composition is too widely varied in this respect, then the markedly more vulnerable person can be either damaged or driven out by the course of group events, or the markedly less vulnerable person in a group may be denied therapeutic opportunities. The most facilitating composition is thus one which is homogeneous with regard to level of vulnerability and hetrogeneous with regard to preferred defense or mode of affective expression.

It is of course impossible in practice to understand prospective patients thoroughly enough to put together an exactly ideal composition. But some attention to these principles of composition often can produce a potentially manageable rather than an impossible composition. The way in which a group is composed is, or should be, the first decision which the therapist makes, and the first opportunity to influence the course of group events. Many therapists maintain that they have no choice in composing their groups, either because the group has been "given" to them or because the pool of patients is already highly restricted (one has only addicts or alcoholics or chronic psychiatric patients to choose from). Whilst it is of course true that some settings restrict one's choice of patients, it is still possible to monitor the composition so as to maximise the desirable mix of hetrogeneity and homogeneity. If this is truly not possible, one can always say no. No group is better than a group which is doomed to failure, thus frustrating the therapist and providing no benefit for the patients. Or, one might choose to work with the group after all, but to revise either one's goals or procedures so that one does not rely upon open discussion as the primary route toward therapeutic gain.

Most groups are neither so happily composed that the therapist need do nothing but watch it develop into an ideal therapeutic group, nor so unhappily composed that no effort can be effective. Most groups lie somewhere between, where the therapist's efforts can make some difference to the movement of the group. The question then becomes "What can the therapist say or do in order to facilitate movement?" As the discussion so far must clearly imply, his role should include monitoring group events and attempting to manage and influence them. This is not his only role but it is an important one, particularly during the formative phase.

Monitoring involves no action. It consists of being as alert as possible to the emerging shared wishes and fears and to the associated attempts to establish solutions. Monitoring requires listening, and listening to this aspect of a group is a skill which can be learned. Because the group situation is complex and constantly changing and evolving, it is unrealistic to expect to feel consistently confident about one's formulations. Indeed, there are times when the group situation is so fluid and unformed that no formulation can be made. The therapist will try to listen in a sort of free-floating way, allowing himself to "hear" not only the content of what is said, but the intonations, pace, interactive rhythms, and non-verbal behaviours of the patients, plus the feelings and internal responses which all this stirs up in him. As he listens, certain possible shared wishes, fears, and solutional efforts will occur to him. A useful stance on the part of the therapist is to try to keep his formulations open and tentative—to regard them as hypotheses which further events will confirm, modify, or disconfirm.

To some readers this may sound too cognitive: a negation of psychotherapy as an intuitive art and a futile and indeed undesirable attempt to articulate the ineffable. This point of view is not meant to deny the therapist his spontaneity, or to ignore those occasions when the therapist may feel cognitively confused but is nevertheless so in tune emotionally that his interventions are exactly right. It *is* a point of view, however, which values efforts toward conceptualizing group events and considers that even "intuitive" interventions can benefit from the discipline provided by a base in a conceptual system.

A therapist who has been monitoring the events of a group still must "decide," either impulsively or deliberately, whether or not to intervene and how to intervene. His general goal is to facilitate the group's movement away from restrictive solutions and toward enabling solutions. However there are times when it is as well not to attempt to influence the operation of a restrictive solution but to allow it to continue to operate. Such times occur when the therapist judges that his efforts will be either ineffective or will create disabling anxiety in the group. At times a restrictive solution is maintained in so adroit and monolithic a way by the patients that the therapist can find no effective way into the situation. His best tactic is to wait until the situation alters just enough to indicate that someone in the group is prepared to listen and respond. (The situation usually *does* alter, given a bit of time, because someone or other in the group finds the total exclusion of any expression of the disturbing motive unacceptable, and provides some indication of his readiness to support a shift away from the restrictive solution). At other times a therapist may judge that the patients need the restrictive solution in order to prevent intolerable levels of anxiety from building up. It is better for a group to talk in intellectual terms than it is for some patients to feel compelled to leave because they feel too threatened to stay. It is better for a group to talk about a television programme than not to talk at all. For while they are intellectualizing, or talking about a television programme or a football game, the patients are also interacting with one another. In the course of this interaction, regardless of its content, little tentative test-outs are likely to occur as to whether or not the person or what he says is acceptable to others. As evidence accumulates that others can listen to what he has to say without the feared shaming or criticism, courage builds up and reactive fears can diminish. So there are times when it is appropriate to allow a restrictive solution its free rein without worrying too much about it.

There are other times in a group when a therapist judges that it is either desirable or imperative to try to influence the group. He is likely to feel that it is desirable when the group has gone on for some time operating on a restrictive solution, when the anxiety level does not seem excessively high or potentially excessively high, when he sees that at least a few people might be ready to shift, or when he becomes concerned that some restrictive solution has run on for so long that there is some danger of it becoming solidified as a persistent way of life for the group. He may consider it imperative to try to influence the group situation if he considers that the restrictive solution operating in the group is potentially damaging to some individual in the group. Some group solutions are, by their character, destructive in impact. For example, scapegoating may deal with a group focal conflict by supporting the shared belief that some unacceptable impulse or characteristic belongs solely to one person. By attacking that person, the unacceptable trait is disowned by all the others. The solution of scapegoating requires for its operation a person who is willing to accept the role of scapegoat or helpless to fight it. It can be damaging to the individual being scapegoated and is restrictive for the group as a whole because it precludes the exploration of the issue except as it is presumed to exist for one person. Another solution which can have a destructive effect is prolonged focussing on one person. Like scapegoating, this can constitute a collusive defense which functions to protect everyone except the one who is the centre of attention from exposing himself. The group's efforts may be ostensibly therapeutic, and the person in focus may have volunteered for the role. Nevertheless persistent focussing may drive a person into a vulnerable and excessively anxiety-provoking position in the group. Again, the therapist may feel it important to intervene.

If he intervenes, the principal thrust of the therapist's effort should be toward reducing fears while at the same time avoiding either collusion in restrictive solutions or the generation of additional fears. This statement requires justification in terms of theory.

In principle and in terms of theory one might assume that a therapist could influence a group toward operating on enabling solutions either by (1) interfering with the operation of a restrictive solution; (2) encouraging the expression of a disturbing motive and thus strengthening its potency relative to the strength of the opposing fears; or (3) reducing the reactive fears and thus rendering the restrictive solution unnecessary. In practice it is the last of these which tends to be effective and the first two which are likely to generate more problems than they resolve. One has to bear in mind that the restrictive solution is functional for the group and operates to keep reactive fears at a tolerable level. It is possible to interfere directly with the functioning of a restrictive solution, but if one does so, one is likely to exacerbate the shared fears in the group and lead the patients to resort to a different but equally restrictive solution or to a still more restrictive solution. Interpreting, exposing or challenging a group solution often conveys a punitive or censorious attitude. No matter how subtle the intervention, the implication is that the group is doing something that it ought not to be doing. Thus, such interventions tend to be experienced by the members as involving criticism from the therapist. Since this is one of the things they are frightened of anyway, it is likely to elevate fears rather than reduce them and force them into adopting a solution which may be even more restrictive than the one the therapist was trying to break up. The most restrictive solution of all which can be established in a group is protracted silence. It is one which above all others is most difficult to influence since it offers so few points of entry, and prevents the very interaction amongst patients which might otherwise lead to the reduction of fears. A direct attack on a group solution is thus a hazardous course.

Interpreting or otherwise focussing on the disturbing motive or shared wish also can intensify the anxiety level in the group. If the patients could accept with comfort whatever impulse or wish is involved in the disturbing motive, it would not appear as part of a group focal conflict. The disturbing impulse occurs in conjunction with a reactive motive or fear, and the patients feel compelled to erect a solution essentially in order to avoid confronting it. It follows that to expose the wish directly will be experienced as highly threatening by the patients. To suggest that there are unfaced feelings of hostility, envy, sexuality, or whatever, is thus likely to be met with blankness, denial, or a sense of having been exposed and now open to deserved punishment. The consequences of focussing on the disturbing motive are either no response at all (if denial is invoked) or the intensification of fears.

The most effective route to helping a group to give up operating on a restrictive solution is to reduce the reactive motive, i.e. alleviate the shared fears. Verbal reassurance is no help in reducing fears. Rather, the patients must see from their own experience that the feared consequences of recognizing or expressing their feelings do not occur. The process is helped along by the fact that the reactive fears which the patients experience are usually exaggerated or unrealistic. That is, the therapist will not really abandon them; the other patients will not shame or ridicule them; they will not be overwhelmed beyond tolerance by their feelings; etc. Thus, if the patients dare confront and test their fears, these fears are likely to be revealed as exaggerated. In response to this new awareness, the fears tend to diminish. As the fears diminish the associated restrictive solution becomes less necessary and the patients can afford to give it up. The process is one of reality-testing. It can occur in various ways and can be helped along by the therapist in various ways. The first efforts toward reality testing in a group often involve very tiny and well-disguised steps. For example, a patient might remark "Some people have trouble holding their tempers." If the response is a unanimous "Only a very childish person would lose his temper," then his fears are confirmed and he is likely to withdraw. The more likely response, however, is that someone will say that many have problems with their tempers, that it is a universal problem, etc. Such a response constitutes a small but significant reassurance to the person making the comment, as well as to the other patients, that angry feelings may be tolerated. It is likely to lead to some further test-out. Perhaps someone will tell about someone they know who has a terrible problem with his temper, or perhaps someone will mention something that usually gets him angry, etc. During such a discussion the therapist may make some comment which underlines what is happening or makes his own position clear. He might say "People often do have a lot of worries about anger, and yet it's a very human sort of feeling to have," or "Everyone here seems to recognize that anger is a pretty universal feeling and a lot of people have worries about it." Sometimes a therapist may have a pretty good idea about what is worrying the patients but may see no signs of any movement toward reality-testing. He may wish to tease the fears a little more into the open. A variety of interventions can be helpful. He might, for example, ask "What would happen if someone felt angry in this group?" or "What would happen if John (a dominating person) stopped talking?" Note that the first question invites the patients to consider the consequences of expressing the disturbing motive while the second invites them to consider the consequences of giving up the restrictive solution. Either may lead to a more direct expression of fears. Sometimes patients directly ask a therapist to state his position: "What would you think of a person who . . ." At such a point the therapist can show by his response his readiness to accept a person despite the feelings or behaviours of which he is ashamed or about which he fears censure.

In general, a therapist can demonstrate through his own behaviour that the shared fears operating in the group are exaggerated; he can reassure the group about their fears by accepting without punitiveness any tiny revelation or expression of a concern or an impulse; he can encourage the exploration of fears. Just how he does this is partly a matter of the situation in the group and the kinds of patients with whom he is dealing. He can ask a question, share a feeling, invite exploration, introduce an interpretation, or summarize the events of the session. Any or all of these can be effective, providing they do not generate new fears by conveying a punitive attitude or pushing the patients too far beyond their current state of readiness.

All of the above is based on the assumption that the fears *are* exaggerated and that reality-testing will reveal this. Does it ever occur that the tentative test-outs of the patients lead to a confirmation of their fears? This possibility certainly must be allowed for, though it does not seem to happen very often. What mitigates against it occuring is the fact that it is in each patient's personal interest to have the kind of group which is accepting rather than punitive. That is, since each patient is aware that talking about his own problems and feelings is the route toward being helped, each has an interest in being accepting so that he can be accepted in his turn. Sometimes individual patients cannot accept some feeling (e.g. "Maybe you don't like your mother but that's an unnatural reaction; I've never felt anything but love for mine.") It is unusual for an entire group to take such a stand unless they are invoking the solution of scapegoating, which the therapist would wish to break up. If the unaccepting response is from one person, the therapist can point this out (e.g., "It's pretty hard for John to see how someone could dislike his mother. Is this a general feeling?") If a general response of shaming or criticizing occurs, then it is likely to be a part of a scapegoating solution. The therapist may choose to deal with this by defining the situation as a problem for the group, rather than solely a problem of the person being scapegoated (e.g., "There seems to be an assumption here that it is only Harry who has ever had this feeling."

Sometimes the confirmation of the patient's fears can come inadvertently from the therapist. Interventions which are experienced as punitive can intensify fears or generate new ones for the patients. Sometimes over-interpretation or premature interpretation can have this effect. Even an interpretation which is technically correct can be experienced by the patients as evidence that the therapist is "on" to them or that any innocent comment will be taken to mean something invidious or that the therapist assumes that they harbour feelings which they themselves are not prepared to accept.

Another way in which a therapist may work against the therapeutic interests of the group is by colluding with some restrictive solution. No therapist, of course, sets out to do this, but there are circumstances in which he might fall into colluding without realizing that he is doing so. For example a therapist might find himself supporting a solution of denial or scapegoating or turntaking, etc., when he too shares the patients' fears. If the therapist *also* fears the consequences of discussing hostility, or dependency, or whatever in the group, then he may be drawn into collaborating in a restrictive solution for self-protective purposes. Some restrictive solutions require the therapist's active participation in order to work. For example, a solution which involves getting the therapist to give advice will not work if the therapist is not prepared to provide advice. A therapist may be drawn into cooperating with such a solution either because he is flattered or because he fears that the patients will not talk at all if he does not respond to their demands for advice, or because he truly believes that it is therapeutically useful for the group. Here, of course, one's theoretical prospective on the group is important, for it is possible that what one therapist might regard as a restrictive solution another therapist might regard as a valuable way of proceeding. For example, turn-taking is regarded here as a restrictive solution, usually functioning to protect the patients from facing competitive or envious feelings about one another, or from facing their yearning for a special relationship with a therapist. Some therapists, however, might see turn-taking as a valuable way of dealing with patients in depth and would, of course, resist perceiving it as a collusive defense or restrictive solution.

Earlier in this article the point was made that it is possible for a therapist, by his behaviour in the group, to spoil the group. To "spoil" a group is to substantially and permanently reduce its therapeutic potential. The two previous paragraphs point to the principal ways in which this can occur: behaviour on the part of the therapist which intensifies the patients' shared fears and drives them to establishing more and more restrictive solutions; and collusion by the therapist in restrictive solutions, thus increasing the likelihood of their being maintained indefinitely in the group. It should be emphasized that "spoiling" a group is not the same as making mistakes. In the complex and rapidly changing situation of a therapy group it is not possible to avoid mistakes. Mistakes can be retrieved and need not have a permanent impact. Spoiling requires that certain critical mistakes be made persistently and repeatedly in the group.

The early sessions of a therapy group can be particularly stressful for the therapist and seem to generate particular concerns. A therapist may fear that all or many of the patients will drop out, that the patients will come but not talk, that the group will get out of control, that the group will be spoiled by a too dominant or destructive patient, that someone will be scapegoated and seriously damaged, or that the group will never do anything but engage in social chit-chat and trivialities. Although experience tends to convince one that many of these fears are unrealistic or exaggerated, they are not mere phantasies on the part of the therapist. They have their roots in the character of the early sessions and in the intrinsic potential of the gronp for destructiveness as well as for constructiveness.

Most of these feared events are, in the language of group focal-conflict theory, restrictive solutions. To drop out, to be silent, to allow someone to dominate the group, to discuss trivial or distant issues, or to scapegoat someone, are all devices which patients can collectively make use of in a group to reduce anxiety. As the preceeding discussion has pointed out, there are good reasons to expect that many or all may occur, and they are particularly likely to occur in the early sessions before the patients have had enough experience with one another to test out the reality of their fears, find them exaggerated, and give up the persistent reliance on restrictive solutions. From the therapist's point of view, the real worry is not that these will occur, but that they will never yield. While it is possible to find examples of groups which died through too many patients dropping out or which never proceeded beyond kaffeklatsch discussion, such undersirable eventualities can usually be avoided through appropriate attention to composition and to one's own participation in the group as therapist.

The above discussion has emphasized the role of the therapist in monitoring and managing group level events. This is not the therapist's only function during the early sessions or later. Nor does it mean that no therapeutic benefit can occur until the group moves past its formative phase. The therapist's role includes attending to individuals and to interpersonal events in the group as well as to shared affects and solutions. Thus, the therapist may direct some of his remarks to individuals in order to emphasise for them the material they are introducing or the behaviours they are displaying. He may function as a meaning-making or a meaning-imputer for individuals as well as for the group. He may point to interpersonal features of the situation—for example, how it is that an individual's behaviour tends to elicit rejection or sympathy from others, or how two persons characteristically support one another or get into conflict. Critical opportunities for interventions pertaining to the individual or to interpersonal events arise along with and among the group-level features of the situation. Persons take a unique stance to emerging shared impulses and fears, or they support or fight against certain solutions. In a prevailing shared mood of anxiety or anger, individuals display characteristic interactive patterns. Sometimes it is to the benefit of the individual patient to point theseout.

Thus, a group focal conflict point of view does not preclude direct attention to the individual or to interpersonal events. It does, however, suggest that when the therapist talks directly to an individual or points to some interpersonal pattern he should bear in mind that he is likely also to be influencing the overall group situation. He might, for example, be supporting a restrictive solution which involves encouraging one person only to participate. Or he might be demonstrating through his behaviour that he favours those who are ready to express personal feelings and is prepared to neglect others who are not yet ready. In a group, speaking to an individual is never *only* speaking to an individual.

A group focal conflict point of view takes the position that certain phenomena are peculiarly characteristic of the small face-to-face group. These include the group's capacities for shared affect, contagion, collaboration and collusion, mutual support for particular patterns of interaction, and the establishment and maintenance of shared norms and shared views of reality. The group-level features inevitably form the context in which the experience of each individual occurs. This article has conceptualized group-level phenomena in terms of the group focal conflict with its component elements of disturbing motive, reactive motive, and solution, and has suggested that an important role for the therapist is monitoring and managing these aspects of the group with a view to generating an optimum context for therapeutic work.

References

French, Thomas M. (1952): *The Integration of Behaviour*, Vols. I, II. Chicago: University of Chicago Press.

Stock, D. (1962): Interpersonal concerns during the early sessions of therapy groups, *International J. of Group Psychotherapy*, **12**, 14–26.

Stock, D. and Lieberman, M. A. (1962): Methodological issues in the assessment of total-group phenomena in group therapy, *International J. of Group Psychotherapy*, **12**, 312–325.

Stock, D., Whitman, R. M. and Lieberman, M. A. (1958): The deviant member in therapy groups, *Human Relations*, **11**, 341–372.

Whitaker, D. S. and Lieberman, M. A. (1964): *Psychotherapy Through the Group Process*. New York: Atherton Press, and London: Tavistock Press.

Whitman, R. M., Lieberman, M. A. and Stock, D. (1960): The relation between individual and group conflicts in psychotherapy, *The International J. of Group Psychotherapy*. **10**, 259–286.

Whitman, R. M. and Stock, D. (1958): The group focal conflict, *Psychiatry*, **21**, 269–276.

Cooperating editor's note

Dr. Sacks is not only an outstanding national leader of the use of psychodrama in group therapy but an outstanding teacher as well. I was a member of a tough, critical professional group, whom Dr. Sacks was able to mobilize, within one evening, to participate in a very rich psychodrama learning experience.

Jim Sacks in this extremely clear exposition addresses himself to many of the questions posed in the introduction to this journal. In addition, if you allow your visual imagination to flow, you may even experience being inside the exciting "warm up" sessions of the psychodrama.

The psychodrama group: formation and beginnings

JAMES M. SACKS

GOALS OF PSYCHODRAMA

Emotional defects are considered to be derived from failures in maturation. To gain access to the mnemonic and emotional remnants of pathogenic experience, regression is necessary in therapy. This regression refers both to the content as well as to the mode of mental functioning of childhood. The patient must not only revive the relevant events but must to some extent reexperience these events in the ways of thinking and feeling characteristic of childhood. Reproducing the identical psychic state which originally interfered with maturation would, of course, be neither possible nor desirable. Theoretically an exact replication could only repeat the original trauma. The regressive experience in therapy is designed to allow the stronger, more mature components of the personality to come in contact with and master the traumatized areas previously sealed off. Psychodrama represents the method of achieving regression in the presence of the adult ego.

The attempt to master the not-present (past or future) by intentionally creating "as if" experiences in order to permit the ego to integrate them, is not merely an innovation of psychotherapy. The same occurs in natural groups of children. Children, however, rarely free associate on a couch but spend their time in improvised dramatic play. In all cultures and without adult instruction they begin these dramas as soon as they can make the distinction between fantasy and reality. With the discovery of dramatic play they are free to test and enjoy an unlimited range of feelings and actions under the protection of the convention of "pretend", of "doesn't count", of "not for real." The capacity to pretend implies the same functional split of the ego as in the actor or in the analysand. One part believes in the game which activates the appropriate emotions while the more mature part of the ego knows better. Through psychodrama we exploit the natural phenomena of dramatic play as an aid to therapeutic regression.

Psychodrama techniques are also employed to rehearse future behavior just as the child acts out adult roles. A clear distinction is maintained, however, between the use of psychodrama to explore the future as opposed to the past. Psychodrama is not a return to preanalytic suggestion therapy or simply an educational device. While psychodramatic contributions exist in these fields, psychodrama is considered here as a tool of analysis.

DESCRIPTION OF THE SESSION

The psychodrama group meets in a small theater-like room. The therapist, called the director, begins with a "warm up" or a structuring of the session to prepare the members for action. In the second phase of the session, the dramatic production, a protagonist is selected who enacts relevant scenes from his past, present or future. He may take his own role or roles of other people. "Auxiliary egos" play the complementary roles and may either be group members or trained professionals. They may play roles opposite the protagonist or accompany him as his extention or "double." In the "mirror" technique the protagonist watches the auxiliaries play out scenes from his life. The director frequently calls for a "role reversal" in which the protagonist and antagonist change their positions to experience the scene from the other's point of view. During the third and final phase a general discussion is held in the light of the drama.

PREQUISITES OF THE THERAPIST

General psychotherapeutic skills are of prime importance. The psychodramatist must have enough self-understanding to keep from unwittingly exploiting his role for personal needs and enough emotional security to maintain warmth and acceptance. He must have available the knowledge which dynamic psychotherapy has evolved but also be free from using these academic ideas as a substitute for empathetic understanding. The rigid therapist who insists on forcing a preconceived dynamic formulation on a patient errs as badly as the under-trained "intuitive" therapist who finds himself trying to rediscover basic dynamic formulations on the spot. Personality defects in the psychodramatist may lead him to overdirect, to become impatient with group defenses or reactive to group hostility against him. While the analyst's passive role may mask neurotic character features, the psychodramatist's personality is more evident. The more active a therapist's role, the more important it is that he be properly motivated.

The director remains in touch with all the group members but must be connected with the protagonist by a special empathetic bond. He needs to be able to find in himself some analogue of the protagonist's feelings both conscious and latent. A director cannot easily facilitate more spontaneity in others than he is capable of himself. When working with a protagonist who cannot express anger the director senses what the protagonist's anger would feel like. The director should be able at any time to say to the protagonist, "I think you would like to do this:" and proceed to take the protagonist's role, expressing the latent emotion in a convincing way. The blend of self-acceptance, knowledge of psychodynamics, emotional flexibility and capacity for acting and directing are hard to find. Many therapists who work well in other modes find they simply do not have a flair for psychodrama. While therapists who lack such a particular talent should probably avoid the method, all those who are drawn to it should not necessarily use it. Psychodrama offers a seductive lure of power and narcississtic gratification. The therapist who takes this bait will harm his patients and himself. The psychodramatist's personal therapy should include experience as a patient in a psychodrama group. The memory of these experiences, expecially as a protagonist, helps him maintain contact with the protagonist's impulses and the defenses against them. The psychodramatist needs to remember how difficult it was to break into new or threatening material. Otherwise he may find himself becoming impatient and having thoughts like, "It would be so easy for me to let myself cry. Why *won't* this patient just let himself go?!"

The director should have had a wide range of experiences as an auxiliary ego to help him know how and when to call in auxiliaries and what they can or cannot do for his protagonist.

THE SETTING AND DURATION

The classical psychodrama stage consists of three concentric circles ascending by steps to the central action area. The lower levels serve as symbolic transition points between the here and now reality of the group and the "as if" world of the drama. The lower levels also provide continuous walkways on which the participants may pace without changing direction. In this way continuous horizontal movements can be represented in a limited space. A vertical dimension is provided by a balcony which rises behind the stage. The chairs are normally grouped in front of the stage theater style but are movable so that the seating pattern is flexible. Props are introduced only to facilitate physical comfort or to extend the range of behavior. Chairs are used on stage but all other furniture is imaginary. A mattress is useful for lying on the stage without getting hurt or dirty. A bank of colored lights with rheostatic controls is required. It should be possible to darken the room completely so that a full range of lighting conditions in both color and intensity can be obtained. The use of lighting is effective in maintaining the focus of attention and enhancing an emotional atmosphere.

The practitioner without access to a psychodrama theater may try to approximate the setting in his office. The vertical dimension, for example, can be added by having the patient stand on a chair. Constricted space, plush surroundings or fragile objects however have an inhibiting effect on mobility. Elaborate decor tends to capture the attention of the patient looking for an opportunity to avoid self-exploration.

The typical psychodrama session runs a full two hours rather than the traditional hour and a half. If the therapist has time and if the group is not likely to escalate demands in a situation with inexact limits the director may run the session open-ended. Evening sessions or demonstration sessions have been run in this way with good results. The director can then allow the session to rise to its natural climax and draw to a close according to the needs of the situation. When used in a marathon group under little time pressure the productions still average about two hours. It is interesting that this is also the length of an average movie or play.

PLACEMENT OF PATIENTS

For each patient characteristic the therapist must usually weigh both negative and positive features. For example, the histrionic patient is sometimes able to exploit this quality for his own therapeutic benefit but he may also hide behind a thespian pose. A professional actress began by "showing off" like an exhibitionistic child. After her double exposed her manipulative motives she went through a painful period of silence lasting several months. When she came out of this she started to use her acting ability in a more genuine way and progressed faster than she might have in another kind of group. Other extroverted artificial personalities offer almost intractable resistance feeding forever off narcississtic gratifications.

Withdrawn or schizoid patients also have opposed factors operating in their reactions to psychodrama. They may be drawn out of their shells by the immediacy of the drama or they may become intimidated by it. In the latter case they may be more likely to work their way slowly into the conversational pattern of a conventional group. Bearing these factors in mind the therapist can usually make an intuitive decision about each patient. Sometimes an experimental period in a psychodrama group is useful.

Hysterical characters may exploit the psychodrama situation for perpetual disassociated catharses without insight. When the affect can be reattached to pathogenic experiences the feelings burn themselves out. Borderline or psychotic patients who cannot achieve emotional distance usually take well to psychodrama and throw themselves freely into action.

The shy or reticent patient seems particularly suited to the psychodrama format. Such patients are often shunted aside permanently in conventional groups but it is difficult to remain unnoticed as a leading man. The lethargic patient who leans back in somnolence during the session is drawn into the drama. The conventional, over-conforming person can be drawn into personalized self-expression. The utility of psychodrama for the severely withdrawn schizophrenic is well-documented (Goldstein, 1971).

Patients who tune out interpretations are prime candidates for psychodrama. Though intelligent they cannot understand any interpretation especially if it consists of more than a few words. Furthermore, any interpretation of this resistance is itself tuned out *ad infinitum*. Such patients require externally stimulated experiences to penetrate this layer of their defenses so that they can react to the therapy at all. I have seen the tuning out defense suddenly dissolve when the patient is protected by dramatic distance. The same ideas which were not heard in real life are immediately understood during the drama.

Group needs must also be considered. Acting out patients, for example, are more frightening to a psychodrama group than to a strictly verbal group. On the other hand, the spontaneity of acting out patients make them useful as auxiliary egos since the example they set serves as a catalytic role model for inhibited members. Both factors need to be weighed before placement.

CAUTIONS AND CONTRAINDICATIONS

Physical disabilities, e.g. heart conditions, where exertion or intense emotion may be dangerous should, of course, be ruled out before working with a patient in psychodrama. While physical handicap or age may limit participation, patients can frequently work well within the limitations. With the loss of a body function patients intellectualize in order to live separate from the body which they have come to hate. Physical participation helps offset this alientation. Good work has been done with the blind in psychodrama (Routh, 1958).

In psychodrama most of each session concentrates on a single member. While this gives an opportunity for deeper exploration, considerable waiting time elapses between opportunities to be protagonist. If a patient is too narcississtic or jealous to gain from a session in which someone else is featured he may do better in a free interaction group.

Casual observers sometimes express the fear that patients may be carried away by the psychodrama, lose awareness of the "as if" nature of the situation and act out against the other members. The capacity to differentiate between the play and reality is, in fact, surprisingly stable. The only violence I have observed was when a hospitalized schizophrenic not in the scene kicked the shins of a patient taking the role of teacher chastizing his class. An old resentment against a cruel teacher had been revived. Had the director been alert to the premonitory facial and body clues he might have allowed this patient to discharge his feeling within the drama. Psychodramatists who have run hundreds of sessions with hospitalized patients have confirmed the rarity of this problem (Enneis, Goldman).

DISTRIBUTION OF PATIENTS INTO GROUPS

In the running controversy over homogeneous versus heterogeneous grouping the psychodramatist tends toward heterogeneity. Variety in degree of illness, age, intelligence, sex distribution, sexual orientation, race, social class, etc. help to fill the required auxiliary roles. The need for identification through similarity can be filled by pairing off individuals rather than by making the whole group homogeneous (Yalom, 1970, p. 194). It provides useful support in any therapy group but in psychodrama each patient has a natural "double."

GROUP SIZE

Psychodrama groups tend to be larger than conventional groups. The presence of an audience invokes a sense of importance to what occurs on stage. Feelings vary from exhilaration to stage fright. The reactions lend impact and intensity and constitute valuable material for dramatic exploration. On the other hand, the larger the group the less frequently each individual has an opportunity to become a protagonist. For weekly outpatient groups where the members are in simultaneous individual therapy I have found eight to ten members as the best compromise but the optimal number may vary with the setting or special goals of therapy.

Psychodramatists sometimes work with very large groups such as educational demonstrations at professional conferences, sessions open to the public or at open groups in large institutions. Such broad social exposure limits the range which people explore but public self-exploration is remarkably effective in relieving guilt and shame in the areas which are opened up. Neither a therapist's understanding nor the support of one's regular therapy group has quite the effect of communication with an audience representing the public at large. Emotional feedback from such a large group oriented toward a therapeutic goal can also have a beneficial value of great intensity. The largest audiences have probably been the listeners to the psychodrama sessions broadcast weekly on Luxembourg television. While two-way communication is not possible the participants are aware that what they are saying is now being made completely open.

INITIAL INTERVIEWS

In addition to the need to prepare patients the psychodramatist must diagnose and prepare a therapy plan before he places the patient. The director's primary task during the action will be based on the testing of hypotheses about the protagonist's dynamics. The raw material for these hypotheses comes largely from immediate data interpreted intuitively during the session. Material from the clinical history however helps the therapist sketch out a personality structure to which he can relate the detailed material of the sessions. In the group there is no time for narrative anamneses. On the first encounter with the prospective patient the psychodramatist might do best to revert to the old-fashioned diagnostic interview. After an initial ventilation of the presenting problem the patient may be sounded out with open questions about his most significant relationships past and present, symptoms of all kinds, work life, love life, dreams, etc. One to three hours are usually sufficient. If the patient is not upset, taking notes after the initial ventilation may also be tolerable. Group therapists working with many patients cannot afford the pride of the individual therapist to remember everything about everyone.

After the data-collecting interviews almost any number of preparatory sessions may be advisable. A period of individual treatment may enable some patients to benefit from group placement later.

Patients react to the suggestion of entering a psychodrama group in many ways. The eager patients may have frequently chosen to consult a psychodramatist in anticipation of exhibitionistic gratification rather than in any real hope for change. In such cases it may be best to delay entry into the group until their motivation becomes more appropriate. Other prospective patients are attracted to psychodrama by the wish to have auxiliary egos stimulate them out of their lethargy or even beat them into mental health. They are often depressed, dependent and impatient with previous therapists who placed the conversational initiative on their shoulders. Their usual way of overcoming inhibition has been to put themselves in the hands of another person who is expected to force them to open up. Before beginning psychodrama such patients should be helped to realize that depending on external stimulation only compensates for deficiency in their capacity for initiative and does not deal with the cause. The need to be sparked from without may be catered to temporarily. Once involved in group life the source of depression can then be explored. Whenever spontaneous energy does arise it should be nurtured and allowed to grow.

Just as eager patients should be held back a bit to explore their motivations, patients who are apprehensive about psychodrama should be placed without too long a delay. Over-preparation may cause the anxiety to escalate. The therapist would do better to offer a few simple reassurances and place him at once with concurrent individual therapy. Patients who are greatly frightened by the prospect of psychodrama should, of course, never be met with insistence but their reluctance explored in the individual sessions.

Some patients ask for prior information about the group in order to insulate themselves against anything unexpected. They want a description of the psychodrama procedure, a personality sketch of the other members or a review of the group's history. These questions conceal fantasies about what the group will be like. It is useful to explore fantasies before placement. Once in the group, reality factors enter and it will never again be so clear to the patient how transferential his feelings are. A patient may find it hard to accept that he is over-reacting to another patient's hostility, but he cannot deny that fear of hostility from a person he has never met must have an irrational source.

Some patients will express concern about whether the group will know about them in advance. I explain that the group is advised a week or two beforehand that a new man or new woman is coming. They correctly sense that the group will accept the new patient more willingly if they have time to adjust their expectations.

If the prospective patient does not know that the therapist is a psychodramatist there is no need to mention it. Psychodrama is then accepted as simply a part of the group therapy procedure like any other.

THE WARM UP

As previously mentioned the psychodrama session is divided into three phases of not necessarily equal length or emphasis. The warm up, the dramatic production and the closing discussion. In the course of treatment emphasis tends to move from the initial toward the final phase of the session. A new group tends to require a more extensive warm up period whereas an older group can make fuller use of the final discussion. Experience in psychodrama reduces the tendency to fall into obsessive theorizing.

During the warm up sufficient spontaneity is developed to permit the participants to enter into dramatic roles. New patients especially tend to be reticent about entering the drama. A totally unstructured situation leaves maximal opportunity for free expression but the new patient tends to become overwhelmed by the danger of the release of threatening material. This tension rarely leads to therapeutic insight. In the totally *laissez faire* situation the therapist would be completly passive and the group would eventually evolve into the repetitive dynamics of natural groups. The first intervention by the therapist is paradoxically to warm the group up by restricting it. He sets ground rules which offer reassurance against the danger of being overwhelmed by an unrestricted flow from the unconscious and yet allows a field of expression within the rules. If, for example, the director were to ask a new group, "What shall we talk about today?", a likely response would be, "I don't know. I can't think of anything." If, on the other hand he were to say, "Tell us what your sister is like," he would probably get a description. A more inhibited patient might still ask, "What do you want to know about her?" or "I don't know what to say." The therapist might then need to limit the patient even more in order to free him by some such direction as, "Has she been pretty popular with the girls in high school?", etc. The tactic of the warm up period is to offer as much structuring as the group requires but as little as is necesssary to be effective. As the warm up proceeds the structuring diminishes. Similarly, as the group becomes more experienced over a series of sessions the extent of the initial structuring deceases.

The group may defend itself not only by silence, but also by falling into stereotyped patterns. The warm up procedures serve not only to enable the group to begin to talk but also to move in a therapeutic direction. If the group falls into an unending flow of self-congratulation it may be wise to suggest that each member restate his goals in therapy.

Innumerable procedures for the initial warm up have been described. Many of the "therapy game" and "self-confrontation techniques" are essentially similar (Malamud and Machover, 1965). The following techniques are typical but, of course, there are many others and every director invents some.

1. The circle warm up

(Weiner and Sacks, 1969). The group is seated in a tight circle and asked to lean forward and look down. The forward posture within the circle imparts a sense of belongingness shifting the focus of attention from the environment to the inner life. Soft light or darkness enhances the mood. The group is then asked to speak in turn giving one sentence each on a topic provided by the director. Members may "pass" if they wish. After each full circuit the director gives another topic. Depending on the group and its characteristic defenses he may choose concrete or abstract topics. With new groups or with children, adolescents or constricted adults he might begin with a highly restrictive topic as "How I felt about the moon landing," as a way of establishing fluency. Typically with adults the director will begin with topics more conducive to immediate personal involvement, e.g. "A feeling I had today"; "Something I like about myself"; "Something I don't like about myself"; "How I feel at this moment"; "Something that happened when I was a child"; etc. After the warm up takes hold topics can be suggested which might have been too threatening at the outset, such as, "What bothers me about my mother"; "What bothers my spouse most about me"; etc. The topics can be chosen to fit specific areas known by the director to be of particular importance to the group, e.g. "How I feel when I come off drugs"; a specific situation, e.g. "How I felt when the therapist took a winter vacation"; or a specific individual, e.g. "How I feel when someone in the group cries" (to aid the reality testing of a patient afraid to cry because of fear of ridicule). The director may wish to allow the same topic to go for several rounds to allow the responses to deepen. As the warm up progresses he can slowly withdraw his guidance. He may ask for the topics to be suggested by the group. The person suggesting the topic is then the first to give his comment. The group will often accept a topic such as "the wildest masturbation fantasy I ever had," if it comes from another group member which it would reject if it came from the director. The structure may be loosened even further by dropping the topics and allowing each person to say whatever he wants in one sentence when it is his turn. If this suggestion is made prematurely the statements slip back into defensiveness but if the group is well warmed up the statements grow in significance and enter areas that the director could never have predicted no matter how well-chosen the topics. It is often fruitful to allow this procedure to run for a considerable length of time. In the later stages of the Circle Warm Up the statements begin to relate loosely to preceding statements, one person's honesty embolding another and reminding him of related ideas. A kind of group free-association develops which the director may interrupt at any time to select a protagonist and to move into the drama.

Several variations of the physical arrangement can be adopted. If the mood of the group turns depressive or tender it often helps to suggest taking hands in the circle. The group may be seated in alternating sex order if homosexual anxiety might be expected to make the hand-holding have an inhibiting rather than a freeing effect. The geometric shape of the circle which the group forms is important. A member may place his chair back just enough to give the feeling that he is not an equal. A variation used in groups able to handle more intimacy is to lie in a circle on a carpeted floor with shoulders in contact at the center. In a low light or darkness this position encourages closeness.

The use of the one sentence round-robin method is a help in establishing universal involvement. Even the shy patient can usually manage one sentence while monopolizers and narrators must come to the point. Everyone remains attentive because the speeches are short and easy to listen to and because it will soon be their turn to speak. The procedure works best if the therapist can remain silent most of the time. The rules of the warm up are set and allowed to run. Even if the members break the rules, speaking more than one sentence or out of turn, it is best not to repeat the rule unless the warm up threatens to disintegrate.

2. The invisible painting (Lenchner)

The group is asked to paint pictures in pantomime. This physical warm up helps the verbally inhibited members to get involved. After a time several members are asked to describe their paintings. They then enact a scene based on the painting and its associations.

The content seems vague and unrelated to life problems at first, but material of more obvious relevance emerges. The psychodramatist soon realizes that emotional release is associated with specific material and that discussing abstractions is usually defensive. The tendency is often to press the patients to be too specific too soon. During the warm up it is wiser to permit a free flow of all generalizations from cliches to poetry. If pressured to release the specifics people will tend to avoid difficult areas entirely. If they can speak in more general terms they often reveal clues about otherwise hidden matters. These clues can be followed up later in the concrete dramas.

3. The non-verbal warm up (Fine, 1959)

The group is asked to remain silent for a stated period, perhaps fifteen minutes. It may also be suggested that they mill about or try to communicate without words. At the end of this time they are asked to describe what happened, how they felt and what they thought during the silence. Pressure to talk certainly inhibits many patients. The pressure not to talk at first reduces this anxiety but later builds up the counter-wish to talk which is then suddenly released.

4. The empty chair technique (Lippitt, 1958)

In this method each person is asked to imagine someone sitting in an empty chair placed on the stage. The activity is entirely intrapsychic. The members participate only mentally and so cannot be judged. Next the group is asked if anyone was unable to form an image. Asking the question in a negative form requires active volunteering from the members who were presumably too inhibited even to engage in the mental activity. Rather than volunteer many members prefer to fulfill the lesser task. If no one volunteers the group has put itself on record as having universally accomplished the task and can be asked about their precepts. If anyone does volunteer the imaginative block can be explored. The director may then choose several likely candidates and ask them whom they saw in the chair. Further questioning elicits how the imagined person was seen, his posture, clothes, facial expression, etc. Soon most members are ready to take the next step of entering into physical action by "showing" the others how they saw the person. They are asked to sit in the chair in the position of the person they saw. At first they are not required to speak. Finally the person sitting in the chair is addressed with some simple question such as, "What is your name?" Once they answer they have already entered into the role and the drama can be developed from this start.

5. The magic shop (Moreno, Z. T., 1959)

An auxiliary is appointed take the role of the shopkeeper in a hypothetical shop that sells anything. The members visit the magic shop and negotiate. The shopper has only a limited time and will not be able to return. The shopkeeper has in stock drugs, sexual potency, beauty, money, academic degrees, love, etc. In the bargaining the shopkeeper tries to get something valuable that he will be able to use for barter with others. He may ask for ten years of life, the shopper's fertility, etc. The drama reveals the quantitative relationship of the patient's values and needs. From these fantasies it is not difficult to move the scene from the hypothetical to related real material.

In most groups there is a tendency for certain members to dominate and others to be squeeeed out. Some of the quieter members are consciously happy to avoid working on their problems, others resent being "ignored" while at the same time they cannot break in. A more routine approach to this problem would be to have the group describe and explore the reasons for this pattern of participation. This time consuming diversion usually fails to change the pattern and it becomes more productive to use a structured warm up to help overcome the resistance.

THE NEW MEMBER

Except for very frightened initiates it seems best to allow new patients entering an ongoing group to fall into natural sociometric roles with a minimum of introductions or special hospitality on the part of the therapist. Groups are usually cordial to a new patient.†

† For a contrary observation see Yalom. (op. cit. P.280 f.f.).

They feel judged by him as a group and they identify with his insecurity. The first session for a new patient is often a fruitful one for the old patients who reveal more than usual about themselves in order to set an example of openness. The need to fill him in on everyone forces the other patients to summarize their condition. They have often avoided this since summarizing prevents the usual "beating around the bush." When the old patients feel the new member to be sufficiently wooed they gently ask a little about him. Then they commonly wait for several sessions before expecting him to take much direct part in the drama. At first they choose him for easy auxiliary roles and finally to be the protagonist. Realignments of group structure take place as the new member becomes integrated. These changes act as a spur to the group which has come to social equilibrium raising a myriad of reactions for examination. Such feelings between group members can be dealt with either by direct confrontation or psychodramatically. The psychodramatic approach is especially helpful when patients lack the courage to voice their feelings about each other directly. In this technique the protagonist expresses his feelings to an auxiliary ego even though the real person is in the room. The protagonist is freed by the structure of the drama. Whenever this device is used to facilitate intragroup communication it is vital to provide the person who has been the object of those feelings with an opportunity to respond.

THE PATIENT AS THERAPIST

Every patient will be called upon from time to time to perform in the role of an auxiliary ego and thus be a co-therapist as well as a patient. The delibilitating effect of the "sick" role is reduced when the patient is sometimes the helper as well as the helped. In relation to the therapist he sees himself also as a student of learning psychodrama skills rather than only as the patient needing to be cured by the doctor. In the therapeutic role patients come to understand dynamic formulations which would otherwise be resisted. After seeing the mechanism in others they can sometimes apply the same idea to themselves. The patient-therapist role also helps to strengthen the capacity for responsibility toward others. In other therapy methods narcissistic characters often disguise their self-centeredness as appropriate to their patient status, but in psychodrama the patient who resents the giving role is soon seen as such. Under group scrutiny this symptom becomes ego-alien and can be explored.

Some patients may exploit this aspect of psychodrama and restrict themselves to the "therapist helper" role to avoid facing their own problems or to feel superior. If the group does not bring this up for discussion the therapist should.

TRAINING THE GROUP TO TAKE AUXILIARY ROLES

The use of auxiliary therapists to represent roles of absent people is peculiar to psychodrama. Some directors use specially trained therapists rather than group members. Such multiple therapy is necessary with hospitalized patients who cannot learn the skills but in other settings the advantages are very great for the group to act as each other's auxiliary egos. The presence of professional auxiliary egos raises difficult status problems in the group (Seabourne, 1970).

When working with a naive group the therapist must act not only as director but as a trainer of auxiliary ego skills. He may break in occasionally with actual didactic explanations. Direct teaching becomes less necessary as the group becomes proficient. Patients come to take pride in their insight and their ability at timing. They develop their capacity to sense the ego strength of the protagonist and to introduce interpretations via their roles. In the auxiliary roles they learn to maintain an open line of communication with the director, with the group as a whole, with their own emotions and with the different facets of the protagonist's personality. They learn to work with mind, body and emotions, improvising freely while observing the director's overall strategy. They learn to sense the counter-role which the protagonist expects from the antagonist. Some patients become extremely talented.

It is usual for the protagonist to select his own auxiliaries. When a new member is selected in this way he usually finds it easier to get started than when he is chosen by the director. If a new patient is ignored by the group the director may need to call him in before he becomes entrenched in a non-participatory role.

To avoid confusion the patient-auxiliary may be oriented to his role with a single point of concentration, i.e. his aim or purpose in the scene. The goal which the character seeks should be explicit without indication as to tactics. Clarity about *what* to do combined with maximum freedom to do it usually makes for the most inventive exploitation of the role. The director might say to an auxiliary taking the role of a father, "Get your son to get a job." The auxiliary may first suggest the idea to his son in a pleasant way. If that is not effective he may shout; that failing he may move on to hostile silence, pleading, threats or guilt producing mechanisms. After a role reversal the auxiliary will learn to use the tactics of the actual father. Directors sometimes assume auxiliary roles as a teaching device or because a performance is required which no one in the group can provide. Sometimes a protagonist asks the director to take a role. The therapist's direct participation also has its disadvantages. It risks intimidating the patients into feeling that they cannot take the auxiliary roles well enough and removes the director from his objective observation post.

RESISTANCE AND TRANSFERENCE

In contrast to non-psychodramatic therapies resistance tends to start more strongly and later drops to a more moderate role. The initial resistance reflects the group's anticipation that the acting-out may mobilize feelings that could be intellectualized indefinately in verbal therapy. Resistance and anxiety diminish as the therapeutic factors take effect. Patients find that they can loosen control at their own speed. They discover the protection of the "as if" quality of the drama. They see other patients expose sensitive feelings and receive group support. They gain self-esteem from their auxiliary ego work.

In the traditional analysis of transference the therapist sometimes finds himself trying to prove that he, the analyst, is not the real source fo the patient's feelings. In a negative transference the patient hears only the evil authority figure defending himself and trying to prove that the patient's feeling is not justified. When the therapist attempts to point out the distorted reaction to his interpretation the same resistance arises in infinite regress. The analyst cannot get out of the transferential role enough to make effective contact about the transferential role. The psychodamatist can break this cycle by exploring the transference through drama. Feelings can be clarified by scenes in which the patient speaks to an auxiliary ego taking the part of the therapist. Sometimes he can speak more freely in such a drama than in direct confrontation. Next, he may reverse roles so as to express what he imagines the therapist feels toward him. In this role he may discover that these emotions are indeed his own and that he has been projecting onto the therapist. Feelings aroused in these scenes can be used as memory clues to previous experiences. When these related early scenes are reenacted the patient often becomes aware of the displaced quality of the original transference without having been told explicitly. This method of tracing can also be applied to the distortion in reactions to other group members and to figures in current life.

FUTURE

Certain recent general cultural trends seem to have influenced our forms of psychotherapy. We have moved from will power to spontaneity; from the "then and there" to the "here and now"; from the word and thought to the act; from the product to the process; from the rugged individual to the commune—the small integrated group. As early as 1923 J. L. Moreno was predicting and advocating these very changes. To what extent he prognosticated correctly and to what extent he influenced these historical trends is not easy to evaluate. In any case the epitome of these trends for him was to be found in psychodrama. Certainly his influence was deeply felt both in psychiatry and in drama. (His theatre of spontaneity and living newspaper spawned audience participatory and improvisational theatres in England and the U.S.) Some of these trends have been exaggerated and distorted in certain excesses of the encounter group movement which cheapen human feeling by forcing it and which under-rate our cognitive functions. Perhaps when the mindless orgy is over more therapists will look again at what Moreno had in mind with psychodrama when he triggered the group psychotherapy explosion.

References

Enneis, J. Personal communication.

Fine, L. J. (1959): Non-verbal aspects of psychotherapy. In J. L. Moreno and J. Masserman (Eds.) *Progress in Psychotherapy*, Vol. 9, New York: Grune and Stratton.

Goldman, E. Personal communication.

Goldstein, J. A. (1971): Investigation of doubling as a technique for involving severely withdrawn patients in group psychotherapy. *Journal of Consulting and Clinical Psychology*, **37**, 155–162.

Lenchner, L. (1973): Personal communication.

Lippitt, H. (1958): The auxiliary chair technique. *Group Psychotherapy*. **2**, 8–32.

Malamud, D. I. and Machover, S. (1965): *Toward Self-Understanding: Group Techniques in Self Confrontation*. Springfield, Ill., Thomas.

Moreno, J. L. (1923): The theater for spontaneity. *Psychodrama Monograph* 4, New York: Beacon House, 1944. Translated from *Das Stegreiftheater*, Potsdam: Keipenhauer.

Moreno, Z. T. (1959): A survey of psychodramatic techniques. *Group Psychotherapy*, **12**, 5–14.

Routh, T. A. (1958): Psychodrama and the blind. *Group Psychotherapy*, **11**, 213–215

Seaborne, B. (1970): The role of the auxiliary. In Blatner (Ed.), *Psychodrama, Role-Playing and Action Methods*, mimeo.

Weiner, H. B. and Sacks, J. M. (1969): Warm up and sum up. *Group Psychotherapy*, **22**, 85–102.

Yalom, I. D. (1970): *The Theory and Practice of Group Psychotherapy*, New York: Basic Books.

Cooperating editor's note

Dr. Samuel Hadden is one of the grand old men in group therapy. For years he has been active in AGPA (American Group Psychotherapy Association) often leading workshops on the homosexual group.

Dr. Hadden's writing approach is an informal, rambling, personal statement of how he does his therapy. He does not derive his clinical techniques from any systematic theory, e.g. psychoanalytic or social psychological, but from his decades of successful common sense practice. A kindly, paternalistic approach to the homosexual man, reflected throughout his article, is probably a vital dimension of therapeutic change in his groups.

The homosexual group: formation and beginnings

SAMUEL B. HADDEN

In the first issue of the International Journal of Group Psychotherapy (1951) I presented an article on the utilization of group Psychotherapy in General Hospitals in which I emphasized the necessity of proper preparation of patients for the group. When I began to use this approach to patients' problems in 1937, group psychotherapy was not a familiar procedure and some patients, when informed they would be treated with others in a group, felt they were being rejected and did not report. Those who did report often dropped out and I soon appreciated the necessity of more careful preparation. I assured patients that after joining the group they would still be privileged to see their therapist in private sessions whenever they requested. They were informed that we were bringing them into a group because we had found that free discussion of conditions such as theirs responded well to this approach. We did this because very soon after beginning the use of a group approach we were thoroughly convinced of its unique benefits. After these measures were taken very few patients failed to report and our drop-out rate was insignificant. Consequently, when we began to treat the homosexually-oriented, we were careful in preparing them for group treatment to avoid an experience they could interpret as one more rejection.

Practically all of our experience in the treatment of the homosexually-oriented has been with private practice and the majority have been educated beyond the high school level with most being college graduates or students. A substantial number have had Doctoral degrees; some in medicne. They ranged in age from their teens to their fifties with only a few in the latter bracket. Most have been in the twenty-five to thirty-five range and it is with this group that greater success can be anticipated.

All patients who are incorporated into a homosexual group are seen a varying number of times individually until I have a reasonably accurate understanding of the dynamics of their particular problem and their attitudes towards it. When we feel confident that we can protect them when protection is necessary in sessions, and that we can focus additional attention on certain aspects of discussion to be helpful to each individual, we inform them of our intention to bring them into a group. Before we do, however, we discuss their admission with the group so that at the time they join they know that the group already has some information about them and that they have been accepted as a member. On entering the group the individual knows each member has a homosexual problem and customarily we give him a very brief description of the members of the group into which he is introduced.

In preparing patients for admission to a group made up exclusively of homosexuals, it is often necessary to deal with a variety of anxieties. Some fear that they might be recognized by others in the group and thus jeopardized. Most are easily convinced that should they be recognized there is no more likelihood that their interests would be jeopardized than that they would betray the confidences of members that they might recognize. Some fear that a liason might develop with someone in the group. but they can be assured that the members of the group are joined in an effort to move toward more acceptable orientation. While the group is made up exclusively of those who have a homosexual problem, we make few demands about their behavior outside the group but we emphasize that getting together outside is to be reported to the group and any information they may acquire about a member is to be reported. Often there is objection to this demand as "squealing," but we point out that this is not a social group and revealing this information is helpful to the individual and the group as a whole. Any form of anxiety revealed must be dealt with appropriately and all aspects of the therapy group must be freely discussed to dismiss any reserve one might have before entering.

I feel that when the therapist is convinced of the value of the group approach, results superior to those obtained in individual therapy can be obtained. This does not imply that patients cannot be treated effectively on an individual basis; nor do I believe that they cannot be treated in groups that are not made up exclusively of homosexuals, because I admit patients with homosexual orientation into groups made up of members with a variety of disorders and I treat some successfully on an individual basis. Most of those I have treated on an individual basis are those who would not agree to join a group. The homosexual I admit to a mixed group is one who has acquired sufficient ego-strength in individual treatment to tolerate any rejection that he might experience when the nature of his problem is revealed. In order to be assured of success it is desirable that the mixed group to which a homosexual is referred should also have moved on to a considerable degree of maturity and have the ability to accept one with a symptom which is regarded by society as reprehensible. I would not put a homosexual in a beginning mixed group. The tolerant and acceptant attitude of the therapist will assure the acceptance of the homosexually-oriented as one who has a legitimate right to their understanding and help when the group itself has matured.

In our preliminary contacts with all homosexually-oriented patients we inform them that we do not believe that there is such a thing as an individual who is "a homosexual." We regard homosexuality as one symptom in a person who is maladjusted and that the emphasis in treatment will be on overall personality growth. As additional ego-strength and understanding of those mechanisms which brought about their homosexual orientation are developed we can anticipate eventual change to a heterosexual pattern.

We emphasize that homosexuality as a symptom is experientally determined and that those experiences which are most significant in determining a homosexual orientation most often occur in the early years of life. Thorough exploration of early life experiences will bring about insights that will contribute to change. We comment, too, that being deprived of some experiences might be equally significant.

In reviewing the experiences of the homosexually-oriented, while there are a suprising number of traumatic experiences which contribute to maladjustment, we stress the fact that the actual homosexual acts are an ego-protective mechanism utilized to offset the feelings of loneliness, rejection and alienation.

In their early lives we consistently find that there has been difficulty in individuation. Fear has been activated in parental relations because of dominance and control by a mother who was threatening and castrating or by a mother who has been sweet and seductive and equally effective in dominating and castrating the child. Likewise, a threatening and rejecting father or one who is weak or absent does not assist in providing for an appropriate identification.

Another traumatic experience in early life that is common in the history of the homosexually-oriented is inter-parental conflict which confuses the child and makes a proper identification precarious.

The most consistently revealed experience in the formative years is the deprivation of peer play in the pre-school years (Hadden, 1966, 1967). The unstructured play of children from the toddling period to about five involves much physical contact in which there is hugging and embracing, running and falling and rolling around on the ground or floor. There is much screaming and laughter accompanying this rough and tumble scrambling play and being a part of such play gives one the feeling of belonging to the group. Inevitably in this type of play there are going to be little accidents as one is bumped and hurt. Seldom are they serious. When one of the group cries out in pain the play invariably stops and the buddies show great concern. The injured one, as the pain subsides is usually the one to resume the rough and tumble play. From this kind of activity one acquires the feeling of being accepted and belonging. One also acquires agility and coordination which is helpful in sport and other group activities that come along later.

The child deprived of this type of play activity may shrink from close and intimate relations, and his ability to make trusting affectionate relationships will be handicapped. He is so frequently a loner because of this deprivation that he shrinks from peer play and his maladjustment continues. Homosexuality may be his own way of terminating his aloofness and alienation (Harlow, 1958,

1962, 1966). Harlow's socially deprived monkeys show defects in their ability to make affectionate relationships and adjust normally

Before we bring a member into a group we ask him to agree to attend at least six sessions before leaving, and no matter when he wishes to leave the group we ask him to explain to the assembled members why he is leaving. We emphasize to all the members of our groups that they will remain anonymous in the group and will be known only by their first name.

Since my earliest use of group psychotherapy I often use the technique of muscle relaxation and thought-control as utilized by the pioneer, Dr. Joseph Pratt (1906), in his management of patients in classes in which they were instructed in how they could best contribute to their own recovery. I was first exposed to the technique of "relaxation and thought-control" at White Haven Tuberculosis Sanitarium in 1932 by Dr. Joseph Walsh who was a friend and admirer of Dr. Pratt and his work.

For many years I have utilized a group hypnotic technique in that after the patient has attained a reasonable state of relaxation through voluntarily making his muscles do his bidding, he is directed to demonstrate that he can also assume control of mental functions and recall early familiar objects. In addition to activating his memory, we have him exercise his powers of imagination and concentration until he is able to develop a mental image of a named object. Usually we select a school-room blackboard as the object to be visualized and direct him to draw an imaginary circle on a freshly-washed spotless one; then, in his imagination, to erase the circle from the board and after replacing the eraser in the proper place, to step back a pace and tell me what he now sees there. Most patients report that they see a smudge. We then point out that this answer was determined by the knowledge they had from previous experience that chalk cannot be completely erased with a dry eraser and that their previous experience unconsciously determined their answer and that in all circumstances their responses to particular situations are determined to a degree by the influence of previous experience. We consistently use this recognition of the influence of previous experiences to help them reaize that their own derogatory image was determined by earlier experiences;

many of which they have no memory and of which they might never develop recollection.

This technique we have used in a variety of ways in the group After getting the whole group in a relaxed state we may present a hypothetical situation to which they are asked to respond. They might be directed to regress to certain levels and respond to a situation as a result of which powerful recollection and abreaction may be activated in more than one member of the group. This is an especially effective procedure in the marathon session of eight or nine hours that we hold with groups irregularly.

Whenever a new member is introduced we repeat the demands made upon him as well as the attitudes we have toward the treatment of his problem and its nature. I then have each entering individuaf give a brief account of his problem, its duration, the degree ol activity, how he feels about it, and what he expects from treatment. We inform each member after he has given this brief biographical sketch outlining his problem that no further demand will be made upon him to reveal additional biographical material until he is ready and willing to do so. Subsequently, additional autobiographical material is revealed when he is motivated to do so through an identification he may have with material discussed by other members of the group. Eventually all members of the group give rather meaningful autobiographical data and they are asked to comment and to express the degree of understanding they acquire as they learn of the experience of each others formative years of life.

We emphasize that whenever anyone has feelings about any matter under discussion or even feelings about a member, those feelings are to be brought to the fore immediately, and when questioned about feelings they have about the matter under discussion they are expected to give an absolutely truthful answer even when they are asked, point blank, how they feel about another member of the group or how they react to a particular member's comment and behavior. At such times attention is focused on why they have feelings of the particular nature and in this way a variety of transference phenomena can be recognized, discussed, and analyzed. No one is ever left without thorough discussion of the feelings they activate in others and in such discussions the group motivation is clearly one of trying to help the member to gain insight and not to offend.

My group sessions are held in a comfortable office setting with everyone assembled in a circle. The therapist makes occasional notes on a chart board. Aside from a few introductory remarks made in the very earliest sessions of the group, the therapist does not structure the discussion. A leading question might be asked from time to time and comments and interpretations of material are invited from the group with the therapist interpreting only after the group has discussed the material at hand. Sessions last seventy-five to eighty minutes and are held weekly.

The groups range in size from five to eight and are open-ended. A ninth member is added whenever we anticipate that an advanced member will soon be leaving. This is done because we have discovered that if another member is added to a group soon after the departure of a member who has reached a desired degree of maturity, the group is prone to direct some hostility toward the newcomer and be incapable of absorbing him as quickly as is desirable. If the newcomer is incorporated before the departure of the person about to leave, he or she will be present during the procedure of separating the finishing member from the group, during which procedure the members of the group who have known the departing one for a long time question about material which was previously presented and the various phases of their progress. This is encouraging to all members but most especially to the newcomers.

The fees of the group are on a monthly basis and when an individual is excused for illness or other good reason no charge is made. If holidays occur on the scheduled date of meeting the members are charged but if the therapist finds it necessary to miss a meeting all members are absolved from the charge. During my absence some groups will elect to meet and my office is made available during their meetings and no charge is made for those sessions which I do not attend. Fees are not routinely discussed in the group because many of the members of the group are students or young persons who do not have a consistent income; we make special concessions for them, and they budget some of the cost of their treatment in keeping with their current financial means.

There are many helpful aspects of the group which are unique that I shall mention. First, each member, on coming into the group, knows that he is entering a group of individuals who have the same problem and who are trying to do something about it.

Those who may express a desire to continue as homosexuals are questioned as to why, and those who have the same problem are able to handle and break down the rationalizations which so many have that homosexuality is a very desirable way of life. The breaking down of the rationalizations induces anxiety that enables one to commit himself to treatment and is a helpful mechanism absent in individual treatment. Some persons reveal their resentment on being encouraged to enter the group because they detest their homosexuality and dislike being associated with others who are homosexually-oriented. On such an occasion members of the established group are likely to announce that they have identical feelings. It is seldom that one expressing these feelings does not soon announce, even before the first session ends, that he already feels differently about the group because they are not trying to defend homosexuality but are striving to change.

In the therapy group each individual is afforded the opportunity to relive, in an effective and ego-syntonic fashion, aspects of his life which were initially traumatic. For example, the acceptant, tolerant therapist capable of tolerating the hostile and aggressive assaults of group members can help one to appreciate that all authoritarian figures are not threatening, but may be ready to give consideration to expressions of disapproval and not to retaliate against those who show hostility. In the group one can also work through sibling rivalries and those who have felt rejected by their peers can find acceptance, not by passive compliance to the wishes of others but by being assertive and constructively aggressive so that they are capable of participating in the helping of each other. It is also possible for members of the group to observe progress in others and rather than be envious to rejoice and gain confidence from their successes.

In all of the experiences that one might have in the homosexual therapy group there is nothing equal to the experience of facing the banter of the members who, in a tantalizing but friendly fashion, remind one of his shortcomings and in a good natured way prod him to undergo desirable changes. As they find it possible to enjoy the company of each other without any sexualization of the relationship, they find it easier to enter into more effective relationships with their emerging masculinity.

This teasing banter by friendly and interested peers provides a very meaningful reliving experience. Most homosexuals recognize that they were aloof from their peers in early life and never felt that they belonged. Earlier we pointed out that being deprived of the spontaneous rough and tumble scrambling play of the toddler and prekindergarten period is handicapping. In this peroid of running, falling, tumbling and wrestling there is much embracing and body contact. The closeness activates an awareness that they are accepted by their peers and those who are deprived of this activity are handicapped. The banter in the therapy group provides a similar experience. Criticism and teasing by those who have accepted you and demonstrated their affection and approval can be tolerated and can be very constructive.

Many homosexuals have a feeling of loneliness and aloofness before coming into the group, and when they find the members tolerant and acceptant, they have reported that for the first time in their lives they feel comfortable in a group situation. Comfortable because the group is made up of persons who are trying to understand each other, who are going to accept each others' shortcomings and expect each to try to progress toward a common goal. This group spirit gradually grows and becomes a very important dynamic factor in the foward progress of its members. Many have reported that the group sessions are the most meaningful aspect of their lives and some have even reported that they live from one session to another. As many members begin to progress and report changes toward a meaningful sense of self, changes toward their employment, and other aspects of their daily living, the group is impressed, These revelations are encouraging to other members because they are privileged to learn of the changing feelings others have toward themselves and to see their progress. As one continues to experience acceptance in the homosexual group and to gain ego-strength it becomes an easier matter for him to feel progressively more comfortable in straight groups and the transition from association with gay groups to straight associations becomes easier.

The initiation of a new group presents certain problems that it might be well to mention. Very often the pessimistic attitude that prevails about homosexuality is voiced. At such times it is only the reassurance and the comments of the therapist that can be utilized as evidence that improvement can occur. Of course, the positive transferences that have been present before the patient has been introduced into the group are helpful, but as members begin to experience some change in feelings and the attitudes they have towards themselves and report in the group, the whole group gains confidence in itself from these activities and each helps the other.

In some of the early sessions it is inevitable that there will be some discussion of the attitudes that society holds toward the homosexual and bitter resentments are revealed. Invariably one member might comment to the effect that society has the right to object to some of the behavior of some homosexuals, and a general discussion of society's attitudes is certain to occur with an eventual diminution of the attitude of hostility held toward society.

Thirty-five to forty percent can be brought to an effective heterosexual adjustment and those who do not make a complete reversal of their sexual pattern consistently undergo personality improvements which are most gratifying to them.

The efforts of behavioral scientists to improve on treatment approaches to the homosexual orientation are opposed by the militant homophile organizations. They wish to have it regarded as a chosen way of sexual expression and not a maladaptive manifestation. I defend their drive that homosexual acts between consenting adults should not be considered a crime but obstructing additional study of the problem and opposing efforts to help those who are unhappy and disillusioned is ill-advised.

Involved in the militant homophile movement are many clergymen and college faculty members; both of these occupations have long been recognized as havens for the homosexually-oriented.

There has been a compulsory military draft for more than a generation and from its beginning educational deferments have been granted. A high percentage of the homosexually-oriented turn to scholastic pursuits and have been given educational deferments; after their initial degree most have been given deferments to attend graduate school, after which they join the faculty, from which vantage point they are prone to attack "conventional morality" and encourage the homosexually-oriented to organize and demand their rights. Their basic hostility accounts for their involvement in so many "anti-movements."

Those who have been hurt and disillusioned by activities in homosexuality between the ages of twenty-five and thirty-five are the ones in whom we can look foward to the best results in treatment. Age, however, is not of particular prognostic importance. Contrary to common thought it has been my experience that the adolescent and young adult group, handicapped by a homosexual orientation, are difficult to handle primarily because they have not been hurt and the novelty of homosexual activity still beckons. They are hopeful that they can find in it real gratification; consequently, this group is somewhat more difficult to influence. There are, however, some who participated in groups during their late teens and dropped out of treatment only to return later after they have been more disillusioned and hurt by their experience in gay circles. Motivation and persistence are more important prognostic criteria than age.

The conducting of homosexual groups is not an easy matter. I would advise even persons skilled in the handling of therapy groups to avoid treating homosexuality as long as they have feelings of disapproval, disgust, or other negative thoughts for those whose pattern of maladjustment includes the homosexual orientation. I also feel that it would be inappropriate for one who has serious doubts about the efficacy of the group approach to begin. If they have feelings that homosexuality cannot be favorably influenced this, along with other negative views, will quickly be communicated to the members of the group. If the therapist seeks only limited goals to help the individual "live more comfortably with his homosexuality" this I consider to be somewhat self-defeating because this will be sensed by the group and they will not progress to a heretosexual level. I have at all times as MY GOAL for the members, a heterosexual fulfillment. It is not unusual, however, for members to leave the group before they have reached a heterosexual adjustment but they believe that they have matured in other ways and some who have left under those circumstances have returned with the desire of going all the way.

An increasing number of individuals are using the group approach to the treatment of the homosexually-oriented and as others use the method I have little doubt that they will find it to be effective for reasons which they will soon discover. As more homosexuals are effectively treated they will inspire those with whom they have contact to consider treatment and not to accept the statements made by militant homosexual groups that "gay is glorious" and that nothing can be done about their unfortunate homosexual orienation.

References

Hadden, S. (1951): Group psychotherapy in general hospitals. *Int. J. Group Psychotherapy*, **1**, 31–36.

Hadden, S. (1966): Childhood play and later sexual adjustment. *Penn. Med. J.*, **69** (5), 83.

Hadden, S. (1967): Male homosexuality. *Pennsylvania Medicine*, **70**, 78–80.

Harlow, H. (1958): The nature of love. *Amer. Psychol.*, **13**, 12.

Harlow, H. (1962): The heterosexual affectional system in monkeys. *Amer. Psychol.*, **17** (1), 100.

Harlow, H. (1966): The primate socialization motives. *Trans. Stud. Coll.* Phgo. Phila., **33** (4), 224.

Pratt, J. (1906): The home sanitarium treatment of consumption. *John Hopkins Hosp. Bull.* **17**, 140.

Cooperating editor's note

Dr. Edward Scott has been a creative force in group therapeutic approaches to the alcoholic for many years, through his several books (*Struggles In An Alcoholic Family* and *An Arena for Happiness*) and papers, his important position in Oregon, and his activity in the AGPA (American Group Psychotherapy Association).

This article reflects his non-doctrinaire eclectic approach. Not adhering to any one theoretical system, his guidelines for action are always pragmatic, clearly implying "I'll use whatever works." Moving from his basic assumptions about the treatment of alcoholics, he takes into the intimate goings-on of the eclectic clinic for alcoholics which he runs.

The alcoholic group: formation and beginnings

EDWARD M. SCOTT

A therapist's techniques and goals rest upon philosophic assumptions. Usually, the therapist's assumptions or "philosophical world" is never mentioned. I want to relate my "philosophic—therapeutic—world," in the following series of statements.

I. MY BASIC ASSUMPTIONS

There are some alcoholics (approximately 10–15 percent) who will be helped by almost any treatment method. These individuals have committed themselves to sobriety and want another life-style than drinking. Some "belief systems" (form of therapy) conclude incorrectly that their form of therapy "really" did help. *Any* form of therapy would have been as effective.

Some alcoholics (approximately 10–15 percent) cannot be helped by any method of treatment. These individuals are simply not ready, or prefer a slow death. For instance, I know an alcoholic who had aversion treatment at a private hospital, specializing in this kind of treatment; twice to a veteran's hospital which had a medical unit for alcholics; four "tries" at our clinic (state operated out-patient clinic); A.A.; twice on antabuse; once to a state hospital and presently is returning to the veteran's hospital. At this time, no treatment method appears successful.

It is my clinical impression, based on twenty years of working with alcoholics in a variety of settings (state hospital, state prison, medical school, private practice, and out-patient clinics) that the

† The following staff members have made suggestions on this chapter: Joe Colistro, ACSW, Buell Goocher, Ph.D., Bill Mackenzie, M.D., Charlotte Lissy, R.N., Dick DeCristoforo, ACSW, Mary McLellan, R.N., Jill Lokting, M.A., Jack Keener, M.A., Claire Ulstein, Sam Wager, B.A., Gene Taylor, M.D., Sally Engstrom, B.A., Bob and Lois Smead, Jack Donoghue, Ph.D.

majority (60–70 percent) benefit from a particular form of treatment, or a combination of treatments.

The World Health Organization (1967) states:

> The treatment of persons dependent on alcohol, with the best methods available has produced encouraging results. Marked improvement or social recovery has been reported in up to 50-70% of the cases, depending mainly on the underlying personality of the person treated.

For instance, I have in mind an alcoholic who was dry, as a result of attending A.A. for twenty years, but came to our clinic because he felt a need for something more. It was quickly apparent that this individual was schizoid and frightened of his feelings. Our first endeavor was to have him experience some feelings. We had him buy a bag of marbles and bring them to the clinic as a "price" for coming to group therapy. He was able to feel as he brought the marbles to us. We placed him in a group at the clinic which has a special emphasis on sensitivity. The group therapist has reported to me that he is "doing excellently."

Some alcoholics try one type of modality, find it unsatisfactory and search out another form of treatment. Several of our patients first attempted sobriety in A.A. and found it unsuccessful, but have been successful with group therapy.

Some alcoholics (approximately 5–10 percent) recover by a combination of help. Group therapy and antabuse are often needed.

Some alcoholics (approximately 5–10 percent) recover by a conversion experience. For instance, a male alcoholic tried A.A., but failed. He came to the clinic. Later he related, "I learned I was an alcoholic, from both places, but couldn't do anything about it." He left the clinic and later was converted. In recounting his conversion, he remarked, "I gave my problem to Jesus, as my personal Savior. One day I turned it over to Him. Here it is, I said—it's your problem. I felt need for alcohol go right then." This was three years ago. Since all patients coming to the clinic are requested to take an MMPI, I gave him another one three years after his conversion and found major, favorable changes.

Bill Wilson (1971) the founder of A.A., prayed for help when hospitalized in a Manhattan hospital. Later Wilson related,

"Suddenly the room lit up with a great white light. I was caught up into an ecstasy which there are no words to describe."

A second philosophical assumption is that everything has a price. A most primitive paradigm states:

A patient has to "add" and "subtract." Some patients find it relatively easy to subtract ("give-up" something—alcohol, an affair, etc.) but are pressed to "add" something—new thoughts, or feelings, etc. It's my assumption, that most patients find it difficult to "add". In a followup study Gerard (1962) reports that in a study of abstinent alcoholics the following: 54 percent were overtly disturbed, 24 percent were inconspicuously inadequate, 12 percent were A.A. successes, and 10 percent were independent successes. What Gerard calls independent successes (able to grow during their period of sobriety) I call "adding."

The question—is alcoholism a physical problem may be partially answered by the following illustration: A fifty-five year old man who had been successful in business retired at fifty years of age, but his alcoholism was becoming progressively worse. He was certain that it was a physical condition. In fact, he had been to an institution which specialized in aversion treatment and the physician had told him that it was a physical condition.

As we continued, he stated, "I don't like moods." I replied, "Is that physical?" He thought it wasn't. Furthermore, he added that when he went on his "bats" as we call them—(drinking bouts of 5–6 days) "I try to get out of the mood I'm in, and get to a dream world in which I think I'm the smartest man on earth. When I'm drinking I go out of the way to lie and when I'm sober I hate lying. Sometimes, when I'm at a bar drinking, before I get blotto, I love looking at myself in the mirror."

When it was suggested that this was a psychological dependence, he was suprised—yet he elicited no desire to stop drinking. Here, I think we have a combined problem. There is an initial emotional need to drink which, as the bout continues, the physical problems "take over" and the psychological aspects are "wiped out." The process continues. He sobers up, eventually the psychological problem leads to another bout, etc. A theory which champions that alcoholism is a physical condition is merely a partial explanation.

The aversion treatment did not work because he had no desire to stop—because the emotional problems were more forceful.

I have a third philosophic assumption which space does not permit me to discuss at length. In the briefest of outlines, all therapy consists of the following necessary factors: time, sight, relationship and hope (1971A).

With my clinical techniques, I attempt to either maneuver time ("don't dwell in the past so much") or sight ("do you really think you'd do better if you understood?") or relationship ("You can't seem to tolerate closeness"). The "motor" which moves these factors is hope. All therapy to some degree must include hope. The hope that this (whatever it is) will work is essential. Even the behaviorist hopes that his schedules or reinforcements will result in success.

This chapter has the orientations of an out-patient clinic. Reasons for prompting this orientation have been established by Ludwig (1971). He and his associates found that hospital treatment, of whatever nature, is ineffective for the alcoholic, once he leaves the hospital, Second, it's my opinion that work with alcoholics has an out-patient setting. Third, special settings can't be discussed due to limitation of space. Those who are interested in group therapy for alcoholics in a prison setting, or on a work release program, can consult my work, (1973). No discussion for specialized groups of alcoholics will be included; for those interested in group therapy for schizophrenic alcoholics, logotherapy for depressed alcoholics, or inadequate alcoholic, etc. can refer to a former work of mine, *Struggles in an Alcoholic Family* (1970), as well as my other work (1963).

References in the professional literature concerning the problems, techniques and modalities regarding the early phase of group therapy for alcoholics is suprisingly scant.

For instance, in the text, *Alcoholism, The Total Treatment Approach*, edited by Catanzaro (1965), there are only meager mentions of the early phase of group therapy. One author in that text, Thomas, wrote that the members of the group should feel useful and unique, and the therapist should be himself.

Rosenbaum and Berger (1963) have edited a volume on group psychotherapy. In their work, one chapter is devoted to group therapy for alcoholics. The authors of that chapter (chapter 40) merely reported, "Direct requests by the patient for information and advice were more frequently satisfied than in analytically oriented group psychotherapy. Interpersonal transactions of one patient with another were analyzed only rarely, while those described by a patient as going on between himself and persons outside the group, including his wife, usually were."

Mullan and Rosenbaum (1962) write:

> The overall aim of the therapist during the first session is to bring to play all the forces at his disposal that will induce with the group a feeling of closeness, unity and togetherness.

Stein and Friedman (1971) present material of the early phases of group therapy for alcoholics. Several shortcomings emerge from their illustration. Their group was composed almost entirely of veteran patients. One patient had been in treatment for eight years; another patient had five years of both individual and group therapy. Hence the flow of the group dialogue, as well as the interaction, was reflective of their prior therapy. Other criticisms are: little, if any unique techniques or methology emerged; no theoretical positions were taken by the authors. What emerged were typical reflections and comments about any group therapy session.

It is my hope that this chapter presents an accurate view of both therapy and practice, so that the reader gets a "correct feel" for what is presented.

Klien *et al.*, (1964) report on the contrast between what they observed in actual practice of behavior therapy, from the articles written about behavior therapy.

II. CLINIC PREPARATION OF THE PATIENT

Before a patient is placed in group therapy he undergoes the following plan. The patient is initially seen at the clinic by one of our social workers who makes a decision whether the patient should be referred elsewhere (state hospital, crisis unit, de-tox center, etc.) or become a patient at our clinic. Once the social worker decides the patient can benefit from the clinic's program—and the patient tentatively agrees, brief informational data is collected. The interview is terminated by referring the patient to a series of five lectures (orientation) on the following topics: definition and phases of alcoholism; medical aspects of alcoholism; characteristics of successful patients in and out-patient clinic; and, group therapy—how it works; your task, other patients' tasks, therapists' tasks, and goals.

A patient can enter at any phase in these lectures, which are held every Wednesday evening. The number attending these lectures, vary from 20–45. Various staff members participate in the lecture series. We have found the most difficult lecture to be the one on group therapy. We use former patients, who are volunteers at the clinic, to help in this matter. It's our impression that this is an effective technique.

During the process the prospective patient is required to take the personality tests, the MMPI, and the Edwards Personal Preference Schedule.

At the first intake interview the patient is urged to have his spouse join him. The rate of success in this matter is high—perhaps 95–98 percent of the time the spouse comes to the clinic.

Toward the end of the lecture series, a Staffing time is arranged. Staffing time varies—twice in the evening, once in the afternoon and once in the morning—to make it as convenient as possible for the patients.

At the Staffings members of the clinic are present. Every clinic person, whether volunteer or trainee, or employee is required to attend one staffing a week. Prior to staffing we have a Journal club, in which various staff members present current, pertinent literature. These two "events" help to motivate, up-date, and solidify the Staff.

Prior to the patient's entrance to staffing, a summary is given, in order to brief the staff (which varies from 5–15) concerning the patient. Once the patient and his spouse are present, fairly routine procedures occur. We ask: what are your problems? do you, as a couple, help or hinder the problems? and how can the clinic help?

The results of the personality tests are given, which help in zeroing in on trouble spots. At times the problems appear to be intrapersonal; other times, interpersonal. By these methods, we are able to sharpen the differences between personality problems and marital problems—and how alcohol "fits in."

After some discussion, a bargaining process begins. For instance, we might insist, due to the patients' poor prior attempts at sobriety (A.A., aversion, etc.) that Antabuse be a condition of acceptance at the clinic.

If the prospective patient denies drinking as a problem—or that he has any problem—we give him a week to think it over. If he still feels the same, we will not accept him at the clinic. It's our feeling, that this realistic factor is necessary; otherwise, an unrealistic contract is entered.

Some patients need medical attention. If they do not have a private physician, one of our physicians will treat the patient for problems directly relating to alcoholism. All other medical needs are referred elsewhere. A few of our prospective patients desire the benefits of a DVR counselor who works in the clinic. No patient is initially referred to him. The patient must first become an *active* patient, participating in the clinic (usually a month) and then a referral is made to the DVR counselor.

Occasionally difficulties arise when a court referral is made to the clinic as a condition of probation. Although quite agreeable to the judge, the patient "changes his tune" with us. In these instances a letter is sent to the referring judge and steps are taken to clarify the issue.

Patients who insist on laying down conditions from the very start of what they will do or will not do, as well as those who seek an immediate gain (DVR, placate his parole officer, etc.) are not accepted at the clinic.

Space doesn't permit me to expand the potentialities of staffing. I will merely include an example or two, which hopefully indicate my contention.

A fifty-three year old female alcoholic, kept asking, "Why do I drink?" during the staffing. It was suggested that she take antabuse. Her immediate response was, "Oh, I couldn't do that." This was spoken with sadness and tears. I remarked, "You can't give up your lover?" She stopped crying, and after a few thoughtful moments replied, "Is that it! I've never seen it like that! Is that it?"

Remarks were exchanged for a few minutes and then I indicated,

"You don't have to give up your lover completely—you can take an empty beer can to bed with you."

"That," she snapped back, "is irrational to take an empty beer can to bed with me! I couldn't, I wouldn't be able to sleep." Although she resisted for some minutes, reiterating that such a request was irrational and, "What would my husband think?", she did agree to do it for a week. Each day she was to come to the clinic and report "how the night went" to one of the clinic's nurses, the nurse who would be her group therapist.

The next day she reported to the nurse that she bought a can of beer, had her husband drink it, then she washed it out, and took it to bed with her. During the night she had four dreams. The first dream was: "I was going out to buy some beer, and I was climbing a ladder to get the beer, then I awoke before I got it." She reported she usually forgets a dream and "never had a dream so realistic." She got up and smoked a cigarette, and went back to bed with the empty beer can. A second dream was "I was walking down the street to buy a beer, there was some change in my pocket but it rolled out because of a hole in my pocket." Her third was, "I was rummaging in a freezer full of beer, looking for a six pack. I awoke and felt the same feeling about dream—so real." Her final dream, "Took some time before I could get back to sleep, and then I dreamt I was in a bar, there was music and people laughing and I was sitting at the bar and my arms were in a puddle of beer and I awoke." The patient had one dream on the second and third night and none on the remaining nights. She reported, "I put it behind my back, and I felt silly, then disgusting."

Her reaction can be interpreted on a number of levels, ranging from: a silly exercise; didn't work it through; the symbolism of putting the empty can of beer at her back; it got her off to a good start; the technique built a bridge. She was assigned to group therapy, and her therapist reports to me that she is doing a good job. The patient rough typed this chapter for me.

Occasionally a patient is asked to do a difficult task during staffing. Such an instance occurred with a prisoner referred by the state penitentiary as a possible candidate for the clinic's program.

During the staffing, we could reach only a sort of "game of words and promises." I wrote to the state penitentiary that we needed another staffing, in two weeks, before we could arrive at an accurate diagnostic and prognostic impression. We indicated this to the prisoner, telling him to think over for a couple of weeks, a therapy plan for himself. When he returned, the same kind of "game" began. I then decided that a definite challenge must be given, that he get down on his knees, crawl over to a certain staff member and plead for help. He drew a deep breath, crawled over and pleaded for help. At this instance he began to cry. He "really" asked for help. A definite change was observed. He remarked how this technique helped him to "break through" his defense.

III. PERSONALITY OF ALCOHOLICS AND THERAPY APPROACH

A therapist's approach depends in large part upon his philosophical assumptions, his personality, and his beliefs regarding his patient population. Regarding the alcoholic patient, I do not agree with the common professional propaganda, which has become a kind of prevailing echololia, that the therapist has to tread delicately among the patients as if they are "egg-shells."

For the most part, the typical alcoholic has effectively maneuvered others and assumes the same "stance" with the therapist. I do not worry about carefully keeping the tender, sprouting relationship; rather, I employ a realistic approach. The evidence of my twenty years of experience sets the relationship "tone" so that healthy exchanges, reflections and confrontations can flourish.

Evidence appears to support this basic orientation. Jones (1965) on the basis of a longitudinal study (30 years) wrote, "It is not suprising that alcoholic drinking should emerge from among that group of boys where behavior in the school years was undercontrolled, assertive, rebellious, pushing the limits, and overtly hostile." Jones further adds, "The data of this study indicated that this acting-out and assertive behavior predated, at least to some degree, an inappropriate drinking pattern and may be considered a predisposing factor."

For the purposes of the present chapter, Jones observes, "It is important to note the absence in this sample of certain characteristics frequently attributed to adult deviant drinkers (depression, isolation, self-pity, destruction) are not reflected to a significant degree in the Q-set ratings for this sample."

Recently McClelland and Associates (1972), based on ten-year research, maintain, "Men drink primarily to feel stronger," other terms could be employed—with greater accuracy. One alcoholic stated, "I want action; you call it excitement. It's about the same." Another alcoholic male said, "I'd go to a tavern for 1–2 beers; then I'd get involved, and I'd say, 'what the Hell' and I'd stay." It's my impression that excitement is a more appropriate term.

Carkhuff and Bersenson (1967) write accurately about confrontation, when they say, "Direct confrontation is an act not a reaction. It is initiated by the therapist, based on his care and understanding of the client. It brings the client into more direct contact with himself, his strengths and resources, as real as his self-destructive behavior."

I have previously (1970) presented a paradigm for my conceptual opinion concerning alcoholics by:

Ego-syntonic (Character-disorder)	Alcoholic (typical)	Ego-Alien (Neurotic)
1. Acts upset		1. Guilt
2. Little guilt		2. Symbolic
3. Doesn't learn from experience		3. Depression
4. Etc.		4. Etc.

The typical alcoholic is "located" somewhere between being a character-disorder and a neurotic: After he drinks (and hits his wife, has an affair, etc.) *then* he becomes guilty (is sorry, feels depressed, etc.). There is more acting-out (5–20 years) than guilt, and therefore the typical alcoholic has more character-disorder elements than neurotic elements. Accordingly not only appropriate therapeutic methods are needed, but also therapist characteristics.

Some years ago the Arkansas Rehabilitation Research and Training Center (1970) conducted an intensive research on therapists, concluding," . . .that A therapists tended to be better than B therapists in alleviating subjective stress regardless of client diagnosis, and that B therapists tended to be better at dealing with problems of impulse control regardless of client diagnosis.

These data were not viewed as providing consistent support for the A–B interactions hypothesis. Rather, the data seemed to suggest that A and B therapists differ in the areas of psychological functioning in which they effect constructive personality change regardless of client diagnosis." My rating was that of a B therapist.

Recently Roether and Peters (1972) found, through their research efforts, the neurotic patients function best in a group in which cohesiveness predominates; whereas, "anti-social character disorders, in contrast, benefit from the patient's exposure to the main problem they have encountered in the microsphere, i.e. their inability to manage hostility in their interpersonal relationships in real life."

Specifically for alcoholics, the "group mood" or "atmosphere" should not encourage transference nor hostility; rather it should be "a reality atmosphere," in which efforts are made to involve those problems and persons who really are in the patient's life—hence the presence of the wife in the group.

Some of the anger—within limits—needs to be uncovered, or released, so it doesn't come "bursting-out" when the patient is drinking. B therapist is more effective than an A therapist for these goals.

The wives of the alcoholic also need a reality basis, for often they are living in an unreal world. For them an ideal therapist is one who can initially assist them in the release of their subjective distress, and thus (quickly) help them to deal with reality—the alcoholic spouse.

IV. EARLY GROUP APPROACHES—RULES:

Once introductions are over, at the first group session, inform the group that I want them to keep one rule, "You can't do what I call psychiatric swearing." This means none of you can say, "I don't know." By this technique or rule, I can quickly make an assessment of the patient's effort to understand himself and his problem. Therefore, he has to struggle, and the burden is on him—not me. My second rule is that each patient has to "think out loud." This technique enables myself and the group to learn how the patient thinks. Beck (1967) makes the statement, "These findings suggest that a thinking disorder may be common to all types of psychopathology." I have found that one of the most difficult questions to be asked of a patient is, "How do you think—not what do you think about?" Some patients think superficially, "You think a mile long and an inch in depth."

In my approach, the patient is responsible for his behavior. He chooses—others don't "diddle" him. He turns on his own switch (behavior). Perhaps he's unaware of this; it becomes so automatic. A tavern doesn't cause him to drink, although a tavern might be an occasion which he elects to use.

Most alcoholics utilize typical defenses against recovery. I will mention the most common defenses. The first, I term mystification, in that the alcoholic maintains, "If I only knew why I drink, Doc, I could stop." Over the years I've learned the alcoholic doesn't really want to know, because as the sources become clearer, he turns on his "fog-machine," and mystifications again loom. A second defense consists in, "There really isn't a problem." His wife just doesn't understand—it's her problem. A third defense is justification. "If you were doing my kind of work, you'd drink too", etc.

During the first session one or more of the alcoholics asks, "I want to know why I drink?" Typically, this inquiry is buttressed by the spouse's agreement, or by evidence from other sources, or, "I went to A.A. and didn't find out." I used to attempt to answer this question by the usual analytic queries. I found a more fruitful approach to be, "What's the pay-off?" The alcoholic is suprised, and responds, "You mean—I get something good from a hangover? I'll bet you're not an alcoholic," or "There isn't a payoff. Last time, my wife went to see an attorney," etc.

I insist that there is some kind of pay-off (reward). I hold fast, and either the patient or another group member begins to "guess."

"Could it be that you got away with hitting your wife when drunk?" or, "perhaps it was an excuse for an affair," or, "you say it wasn't really you—it was the booze," etc.

Several advantages result from this approach. For one thing, it's better than the "archeological-historical" one because earlier reasons for drinking might no longer explain *present* drinking. I'm interested in the present, not the past. Secondly, the "pay-off" might be so big the patient doesn't want to give it up (subtract) this from this life. Thirdly, this approach stresses that consequences of behavior are more important than antecedent considerations. Consequences (an affair, spent money, etc.) are verifiable; whereas, antecedents are speculative at best. The "pay-off" can be observed, and this is more tangible than the darkness of the archeological digging.

Hard upon this technique, comes another early approach. I ask one member to be "a little less crazy," another, "to be a little less tearful," another "to be a little less angry"—until I've made requests from each member. This approach has a startling effect. It informs each member of the group that, he does have, to a degree, control over his thoughts, emotions, and behavior. Most patients (especially the alcoholic) feel they have a right (almost a constitutional one) to function at their *maximum* level of pathology. I suggest that I can't afford this "luxury," and I expect the same from them. This "slant" is suprisingly successful.

The first session of setting—the mood, new ideas, geared to letting them know that alcoholism is not a mystery, and the benefits are observable.

In the second session I help the members to share more openly by explaining the different selves one has. For example, there are a feared self (you might be a psychotic, criminal, etc.) and ideal self (what you'd like to be); a social self (how you "fit" with others); and a family self (how you feel about being a husband, or wife, or father, etc.). This method allows the members to reveal part of themselves, not to over identify completely with only part of the self. I could give several samples. The following is but one: "Let's say we all have 100 units of energy. If we use up a lot of energy in our feared self, (either denying it, or waiting for it to strike) a lot of energy is wasted, energy that could use toward your ideal self." This helps the patient to "unfold" part of himself.

In the third session, the group reports on the events of the past week, their successes and their failures. From the presentation, I select one or two to "zero-in-on." I begin fussing with their report, suggesting in the case of failure, that a different course of action could have been taken. The typical reaction is, "no way." At this juncture I employ the following: "Tell me six different ways to get across a river." Suggestions come quickly. I ask, "Tell me five different ways to get a job." Other questions are posed. The group is invited to think about what I've really asked them to do. Usually someone gets the correct answer, "use my imagination." I agree, and immediately ask, "Tell me six different ways to stop drinking." Wow!! The answers are slow—and few. When I ask, "Tell me six different ways to get a drink," the answers are quick. I make the point that their imaginations have helped them in keeping their problem going; now we want to utilize their imagination in helping to solve the problem, by presenting alternatives.

Part of this conceptual material is taken from Farber (1966) whose thoughts have greatly impressed me. Farber indicates that willpower (ego strength) requires the input from the imagination; as he states," . . . the will is unable to imagine . . ." I have taken Farber's comments and modeled some therapeutic techniques. I have the group members "limber-up" their imaginations toward the solution of their problems. "Homework" is given and reports are heard the following session.

The first three sessions give the members some tools which they can apply toward the solutions of their problems.

Typical problems occurring in the early phases are the emergence of leaders. Some A.A. members who want to turn group into an A.A. meeting, or paranoid members want to destroy a functioning group are examples. Another problem is what I term collective monologue. This refers to the lack of interactions among the members. They prefer the easy approach of "telling my story." A method used to eliminate group monologue is to have another member paraphrase what someone has just said.

The reader might get the impression that my groups are grim, heartless and confronting. Not really. Interwoven is fun, laughter and humor—even Hamlet has the grave digger scene! Really, alcoholics aren't playful. Supportive of this opinion is the research of Field and Scott (1969) who found, when comparing alcoholics with student groups (On the Stanford Hypnotic Susceptibility Scale, form A), that significant differences emerged; on six items, alcoholics had a lesser hypnotic depth. Several tentative interpretations were given about this. Alcoholics ". . . may be too absorbed in their conflicts to be able to relax fully. Scott (1968) reports that the dreams of alcoholics show that they are preoccupied with problems, conflicts, depression and victimization."

Hence, something must be "added" to the patient's life—play, fun, and happiness. Hilgard (1965) uses the term "play-ego;" this seems most appropriate for the alcoholic and his spouse. Play, of course, is meant to be healthy, recreational play, not destructive unhealthy play. Some patients find this a formidable hurdle—they are so "wrapped up" in their self-defeating life style. Others can quickly respond as can be seen in the following quote from one couple. "We plan something for each evening, and we look foward to it during the day. Maybe it's just popping corn, but it is very meaningful to us."

In another work, entitled, "*An Arena for Happiness*" (1971), I found that alcoholics are not as happy as normal people. Additional information can be obtained from that work, which can be used in therapy sessions.

One of the common problems of these patients are the reoccuring thoughts—over and over, so much so that it can be likened to a broken record. This has the impact of hypnosis. In other words, if a person listens to the same thoughts over and over (like a record) the effect is to be "stuck." The same "music" occurs time after time. One successful method I've emphasized is to have the patient make a circular motion with his hand (portraying) a record, to play over and over the "sad-tune." At times patients will say, "I can't stand it." After this exercise is completed by everyone, a second exercise is to play a "good-record"—any happy, hopeful thought. Differences are noted in each patient's "recording"—one hand symbolizes a "bad tune," the other a "good tune." The question asked: "Who puts on your records—you or someone else?" can be most helpful. The patient can graphically "see" that they are responsible for their "tune" (thoughts)—not someone else. This exercise has been significantly helpful because it gives the patient "graphic-proof."

Recently, a group who had been in therapy for some time was asked to recall their first group sessions. In retrospect, here are some of their responses. This was a good group in the sense of working, married, normal or higher intelligence, not psychotic. Some of their replies were: Tom: "I was hit harshly. It has a 'gut-ripping' experience which was rather cathartic," and, Bill: "I came expecting someone to give me answers, but I found I had to work;" Pete: "I came up tight;" Sue: "I wondered why I was here; this was obviously my husband's problem;" Mary: "I felt mad, but I soon discovered what was going on in another's life was taking place in my own life;" Al: "I stayed because my wife pressured me to stay, and my parole officer was threatening to violate my parole. I also stayed to show that damned Dr. Scott didn't know what he was talking about;" Bob: "I felt intrigued."

As the group becomes more comfortable and workable, "deeper" problems are tentatively presented by one of the group who feels acceptance by the 3rd or 4th session. In group therapy for married alcoholics, sexual problems are often typical. In another article (1958), I have reported on several aspects of sexual problems among married alcoholics. Frequently, the problem of intercourse—withholding, using it as a weapon, or the husband's insistence on intercourse while drunk, his fear that antabuse has inhibited him, and concern about abnormal or unusual types of sexual relationship emerge. The anger and hurt suffered by the wife, of her husband's open illicit affairs, surge to the surface.

Not infrequently, impotence and frigidity are topics of concern and of fear. Former suggested techniques (of the different selves) is a vehicle for assisting the group in this troublesome and painful area. Toward the end of the early phase other therapeutic modalities are added, for instance, hypnosis. My use of hypnosis follows one direction. The direction is toward strength. I have the group, under mild hypnosis return to their early childhood. I suggest that some good times are often forgotten, perhaps those things are put away—like a toy in the attic—although it's forgotten, it doesn't mean that it isn't there. Each patient is asked to return to his childhood, recall and relive a happier, pleasing event. Most patients can "relive" a happy event—which "stirs-up" a forgotten positive relation to the self. It's suggested these positive feelings—are present, but dormant—and they can come "alive" by "massaging them" through this approach. The patient begins to come "in contact" with the healthy part of himself—which can be employed in his struggles toward improvement.

A second hypnotic technique is to have the patient "return" to a former event, which is felt to be successful, satisfying and to "recapture" it. Once this is accomplished under hypnosis, the patient is told to "hold-on" to it, to bring it back to the present, and make it part of himself. In this manner the recent unsuccessful events which have had such a deliberating effect, are by-passed. By illustration:

x — — — — — — — — — —Today
x

Detour

x = Successful Events
— = Unsuccessful Events

When I inquired of one female patient, what helped her in the early phase, she replied, "Hypnosis helped change my thinking. It brought me back to where I was productive and reminded me that I used to like myself."

At times basic questions arise, which gives the group a "bounce." One such topic was "Every one has a price." General remarks concerning this question were made, until I pinned it down to a concrete example, "Would you sell your wife for one night?" Following is a recording from a group of unmarried alcoholics:

Chuck: "No—it's not right."
Henry: "Money is important. If the fellow were a gentleman, and the price were right?"
Dr. Scott: "A $1,000?"

Henry: "But, supposing she says. "We need the money, and I can handle the guy."
Joe: "What would happen after the money is gone?"
Harry: "Maybe, marriage would change how I feel."
Hank: "I've been poor before—but the memory of it would bother me."
Dr. Scott: "Mary, suppose you make believe you're Harry's wife?"
Mary: (Snaps) "I'd tell you, Harry, to go to hell."
Harry: "Money is money. I'll bet others in this group would do it—if they were honest."
Mary: "If the fellow had that much money, I'd go with him."
Group laughter:
Susie: "If we didn't have a good relationship I'd do it for a $1.00."

We then reversed the question—Suppose a woman wants to go out with your husband for $1,000?

Betty: "I'd go for it—if we didn't have a good relationship."
Susie: "It's okay if we needed the money."
Jim: "When I get to drinking, I don't give a damn."
Dr. Scott: "So, you sell yourself out."
Jim: "Ya."

This group began to react to values, selling themselves out—what's sacred, etc.

My theoretical and practical approach to helping alcoholics has the advantage of taking away the mystery and "hit-and-miss" approach, without suffering from a simplistic and, therefore, oversimplification of both the problem and the solution.

Secondly, it gives the patients "tools" (no psychiatric swearing—"I don't know, etc.") from the very outset, without assuming that a long delay (rapport) has to be established before any work can be done.

Thirdly, it is not merely a "techniquing-affair"—with better and better tricks to lean on and props to give. Rather, my approach assumes both the strength and inner resources of the person, as well as real problems. Hence, it avoids the "honeymoon room" atmosphere of other therapeutic orientations, as well as the "slaughter-house" tactics of other schools of so-called therapy.

My approach assumes that, for the most part, life is neither a honeymoon nor a slaughter-house, and techniques are appropriately chosen.

Fourth, it is not only pathology focused—assuming that reams and reams of psychological pus"—have to be drained off—but rather has a healthy highroad as both a means and a goal. PLAY, is therapeutic, healing and necessary.

Fifth, it assumes that the therapist lives the life he models.

Sixth, this approach assumes, and I have yet to see this not an accurate observation—that people have unused strength—that people are not as weak and helpless as they think they are, but have "sold" others that they are helpless—hence no responsibility. Responsibility is freely given to others—the helpers.

The group's development is observable as reports "trickle-in" from what's happening outside the therapy hour, as well as the progress seen during the sessions. It's similar to a football team picking up confidence after each victory as well as learning in defeat. The notion gets across the one thing no one can do is give up! Mistakes, yes—but not surrender.

The deficiencies of the therapy program outlined, is the assumption of a functioning individual. Hence, patients who are inadequate or advanced alcoholics find it difficult to meet the required level of performance.

An important "don't" for a therapist is not to go amateur at the very time a professional performance is necessary. Going amateur means: (a) working harder than the patient, (b) giving in to what he wants instead of guiding him toward what he needs and, (c) "catching" his problems.

An ideal therapeutic relationship is one in which the patient experiences in a directly felt manner, the benefits of his growth. This spurs him on to greater growth. This tapping of potential is pleasing to both therapist and patient.

For the future I envision a city (town) divided into catchment areas (number of taverns, bars, etc.), each with its own "frontline-therapist". This type of worker will be responsible for visiting "his" taverns. He will engage in pool, shuffleboard, and the like. His aim is to instigate "spontaneous" discussions, with individuals, as well as with groups of tavern customers. There are vital moments when a person is drinking, when guarded emotions and thoughts are released, that take months to release, when he attends group at a clinic or hospital setting.

Depending on the attitudes of the tavern owner, Jellinek's chart (phases of drinking)will be posted. This will trigger the information into reality. The "front-line worker" will have at his disposal individuals in the process of working their way down the phases of alcoholism.

The "front-line-worker" will occasionally take a person who has been drinking, home and a family session will occur at the point of pressure—when he arrives home—drunk. Tears, fear, and anger are potentials of foaming into eruption. The "front-line worker" will be at the psychological emergency hospital—the home of the alcoholic.

The front-line worker will have a consultant who helps make decisions and, on occasion, make an "on-sight" visit. The consultant will have at his disposal, a variety of services—hospitals, half-way houses, out-patient clinics, A.A., etc.—all designed to help in timely and accurate referrals.

I see, also, a gradual tightening of the options allowed the alcoholic as he progresses in his alcoholism, until finally he is forced into a realistic, commune type of setting. Kittrie (1971) would term such a proposal as being symptomatic of a therapeutic state—which imposes its therapy on unwilling citizens; as opposed to a welfare state which serves only voluntary citizens. Personally, I see a government functioning in both capacities.

Note must be made of those alcoholics who neither visit taverns, land in jails or hospitals, but are in need of help. For this large group of individuals I foresee a neighborhood program with a variety of graduated involvements—from afternoon therapy sessions for the wives who are either sipping too much themselves or who find it progressively difficult to tolerate a drinking husband. In the evening, marital group sessions will take place in rotating homes of the neighborhood for couples who want help, where the problem is in the early phase. For this "neighborhood program" a skilled worker will be necessary—one who is sensitive, timely, good-willed and yet realistic.

I would like to close with a letter written by a former patient.

Dear Dr. Scott:

Since we quit therapy a year ago, Bob and I have planned to write and let you know how we were doing. We've been busy and found lots of excuses for not writing. I've had plenty of time lately though. I've been either in bed or doing very little the last 2 months because of a ruptured disk. It is much better now and I hope to be all right soon.

Bob is doing so well I can't believe it sometimes. Not one drink and very few times of fouled up thinking. We had a few bad times this summer while we were building our house. We built it ourselves, just hired subcontractors. We had trouble getting a loan and getting the subs to get here on time, but we're quite proud of ourselves for not giving up.

We love living here in the country and have met some very nice people. We have 3 cats, a Saint Bernard mother dog and 11 puppies so we really feel like country people. Bob says the next animal we get has to be a calf so we can eat it when it grows up. The kids think that's fine except for the eating part.

I still have trouble with my weight but I probably always will. It doesn't bother me as long as I don't get as heavy as I was. Bob is getting fat too, so he isn't as critical as he used to be.

Dr. Scott, we think about you and the group often and hope that others are getting the help there that we did. It is great to feel normal and be able to face other people feeling you are equals, not some mess that shouldn't be associating with decent folks. I think we are giving something of ourselves to others that is worthwhile. Our girls are pretty normal now and very sweet. All in all, it's a good life, and we want to say thank you."

Love,
Bob and Pat
(signed)

References

Arkansas Rehabilitation Research and Training Center (1970): 346 N. West Ave. Fayetteville.

Beck, A. (1967): *Depression*. Harper & Row, N.Y.

Carkhuff, R. and Berenson, B. (1967): *Beyond Counseling and Therapy*. Holt, Rinehart and Winston, N.Y.

Catanzaro, R. (Ed.) (1965): *Alcoholism, The Total Treatment Approach*. Charles C. Thomas. Springfield, Ill.

Farber, L. (1966): *The Ways of the Will*. Colophon Bks., N.Y.

Field, R. and Scott, E. (1969): Experiences of alcoholics during hypnosis. *Amer. J. Clin. Hyp.* **12**, 86–90.

Gerard, D., Saenger, G. and Wile, R. (1962): The abstinant alcoholic. *Arch. Gen. Psychist.* **16**, 83–95.

Hilgard, E. (1965): *Hypnotic Susceptibility*. Harcourt, Brace & World, N.Y.

Jones, Mary. (1968): Personality correlates and antecedants of drinking patterns in adult males. *J. Consult. and Clin. Psy.* **32**, 2–12.

Kittrie, N. (1971): *The Right To Be Different*. John Hopkins, Baltimore.

Klein, Marjorie, Dittmann, A., Parloff, M. and Gill, M. (1969): Behavior therapy: observations and reflections. *J. Consult. and Clin. Psy.* **33**, 259–266.

Ludwig, A., Levine, J. and Stark, L. (1970): *LSD and Alcoholism*. Charles C. Thomas, Springfield, Ill.
McClelland, D., Davis, W., Kalin, R. and Wanner, E. (1972): *The Drinking Man*. Free Press, N.Y.
Mullan, H. and Rosenbaum, M. (1962): *Group Psychotherapy: Theory and Practice*. Free Press, N.Y.
Roether, H. and Peters, J. (1972): Cohesiveness and hostility in group psychotherapy. *Am. J. Psychiatry*. **128**, 128–131.
Rosenbaum, M. and Berger, M. (1963): *Group Psychotherapy and Group Function*. Basic Books, N.Y.
Scott, E. (1958): A suggested treatment plan for the hostile alcoholic. *Int. J. Group Psycho*. **13**, 93–100.
Scott, E. (1963): A suggested treatment plan for the hostile alcoholic. *Int. J. Group Psycho*. **13**, 93–100.
Scott, E. (1970): *Struggles in an Alcoholic Family*, Charles C. Thomas, Springfield, Ill.
Scott, E. (1971): *An Arena for Happiness*. Charles C. Thomas, Springfield, Ill.
Scott, E. (Spring 1971): Lecture Grand Rounds, Dept. of Psychiatry, U. of Oregon Medical School.
Scott, E. and Scott, Kathryn, (Eds.) (1973): *Criminal Rehabilitation*. Charles C. Thomas, Springfleld Ill.
Stein, A. and Friedman, E. (1971): Group therapy with alcoholics. In H. Kaplan and B. Sadock (Eds.) *Comprehensive Group Psychotherapy*. Williams and Wilkins, Baltimore.
Wilson, B. (Feb. 8, 1971): *Time Mag*. p. 52.
World Health Organization (1967): *Technical Reports Series* No. 363, Geneva.

Cooperating editor's note

"ZEKE" YOUCHA, a friend and colleague of mine for a decade, is one of those outstanding clinicians and teachers whom too few people know about because he is neither active in professional organizations, nor frequently writes. Happily, I have finally gotten Zeke to write down his often wise and always practical ideas for this journal.

He has applied his psychoanalytic and group process training to a most difficult area, i.e. short term group therapy with very disturbed hospitalized patients. The extremely complex phenomena in this area are penetrated to their essence, all expressed in deceptively, simple language.

Zeke Youcha derives three categories of hospitalized patients, each of which is associated with a different group therapeutic approach. The paper is full of useful "when," "what," and "how to do" suggestions, often within the context of a simple theoretical explanation, and richly illustrated by examples.

Short-term in-patient group: formation and beginnings

ISAAC Z. YOUCHA

On most dynamic in-patient psychiatric services there is a constant effort made to offer effective treatment in the shortest possible time. Due to high costs, insurance companies' policies, governmental pressure and modern psychopharmacology, the length of an average hospital stay has been drastically reduced. On many units four weeks is considered an extended stay.

This reality has forced therapists into the position of attempting very short-term psychotherapy with severely disturbed people, yet group therapy has had little opportunity and time to develop a body of theory, method and techniques to meet the challenge.

For most of the last decade the author has had the opportunity to work as a group consultant in a state mental hospital as well as on a psychiatric unit within a general hospital. I will attempt to present some of the theory, methods and techniques which have evolved from this experience.

PATIENT CATEGORIES

In the main we tend to see three broad categories of patients. A. Those whose psychosis has overwhelmed all ego functions; B. Patients who are psychotic or acutely depressed but who have enough ego functions operating to which the therapist can ally himself; and C. Patients who (1.) are not psychotic (2.) have overdosed, (3.) are on non-opiate drugs, (4.) are alcoholics or heroin addicts, (5.) have made suicide attempts, (6.) have severe somatic disturbances of unknown origin, and (7.) those crippled by conversion hysteria. The major differentiating factor among the three categories is the degree of ego strength and functioning.

CATEGORY A

In this category the psychotic process dominates the ego, i.e. one patient was hearing voices yelling at her and could not accept the idea that they were coming from within. Those voices were real and they wouldn't leave her alone. They told her to put her baby in the oven and that she was the worst creature on earth. She accused the therapist of being one of "them" when he suggested that the voices were really coming from within herself. A large part of this group is composed of chronic patients with process schizophrenia whose illness overwhelmed or stunted ego development early in life.

CATEGORY B

In this category a similar process is at work, but enough of the ego remains unaffected, especially the function of reality testing. For example, a second woman heard voices screaming at her and was sure they were coming from the next room. She ran to the nearest police station for protection. On admission, an experienced clinician was able to discuss with her the possibility that the voices were emanating from within herself. She replied, "You know, that may be true, because when I'm talking to you or am closing my eyes, I don't hear them. I'd rather talk to you. Wow, what the hell is happening to me anyway?"

The therapist was able to appeal to and ally himself with the observing ego in the patient which could still reflect upon herself and realize that something was happening to her. This group is composed of people with a psychotic underlay but strong enough repressive defenses and coping mechanisms to enable them to function when not under excessive stress.

CATEGORY C

In this group we see people whose reality testing is relatively intact and who often have the capacity for self-reflection and insight into the immediate causes of their stress and anxiety. With therapeutic help they can understand intellectually some of the precipitating causes of their disturbances. This in no way means that they can do anything to remedy their situation, but the problem can be outlined and defined in a relatively short period of time. Their behavior often represents a desperate appeal for help. One woman stopped her car on a busy bridge, lifted up the hood of her car and blocked traffic for miles. She was really flagging for help.

This last category includes those with severe neurotic and characterological disturbances whose adaptive mechanisms crumbled under continuous internal and external stress.

Many patients are admitted who fit into category A, but in time with drug treatment, rest, support, good meals and activity group approaches move into category B.

EVALUATION

It is incumbent upon the therapist to evaluate the degree of pathology and ego condition as quickly as possible. This will determine choice of treatment methods and goals. It will be necessary for the entire ward staff to accumulate as much data as they can get in the shortest possible time, and this requires *total* staff involvement and cooperation.

Each category of patient requires a different group approach and it is often not possible to adhere strictly to this approach nor to evaluate each patient so precisely. A broad outline of theory, methods and techniques, however, does offer the group therapist a conceptual framework. This may eliminate the confusion, indecision and lack of purposefulness often seen in a ward staff when it comes time to decide which patients should be put into what kind of a group and why.

Regardless of the particular group approach utilized, all require at least three to five, one to two hour meetings a week. Once a week meetings during a one to four week hospitalization are almost valueless.

A thorough dynamic understanding of each patient's problems, conflicts, ego condition, psycho-dynamics, present life situation and interpersonal relationships, is essential.

GOALS

Clear-cut and realistic treatment goals must be established as quickly as possible. These goals are arrived at through discussion between staff and patients, individually or within the group therapy situation.

Minimal goals might be to 1. reduce the acute psychotic manifestations of the disturbance so that the patient can participate in ward activities, 2. help the patient (with the use of drugs, rest, reassurance and support) to seal over the eruption of the unbearable psychic pain and anxiety which necessitated the use of regressive psychotic mechanisms of defense. This implies an attempt to substitute and encourage repressive devensive mechanisms, i.e. obsessive-compulsive or denial devices, in place of the psychotic ones the patient had resorted to. This is done when the goal is not to uncover and resolve the sources and nature of the anxiety-producing conflicts, but instead to enable the patient to reestablish previous non-psychotic levels of functioning. For example, a twenty-six year old mother of two, employed as a school teacher, believed that her family was under surveillence by enemy powers and was going to be murdered at any moment. After four days of drug therapy and exposure to a benign therapeutic community and activity group approach (to be described below) the delusion ceased to be active. It was replaced by an obsessive-compulsive concern about performing all of her chores perfectly. Any attempt to deal with her rage at her husband, her early deprivation as a child, her displacement of rage at her mother onto her husband, was met with agitation, confusion and an acute exacerbation of the psychotic delusion.

No one could establish an alliance with an intact psychotic-free portion of her ego. (She obviously would fit into category A.) Thus, our minimal goals were to accept and support severe compulsive-obsessive repressive defenses in place of her previous regressive psychotic ones.

Intermediate goals with such a patient might have been to help her recognize that she was unhappy in her marriage and her job, that her husband frequently hurt and enraged her and that this rage was attributed to others. It could have been approached on a behavioral level by helping her to express anger to fellow patients and ward staff which she never did, even when sharply provoked. In a group situation we could have dealt with why she was not even aware of feelings of irritation at a most provocative group member.

More extensive, or maximum goals would have included couple, group and individual therapy with the aim of working on her transferential distortion of her husband, her fear of homicidal rage, its sources, etc. The group would have been utilized to examine how she dealt with her major affects and to help her discover other less destructive modes of affectual expression.

We chose not to select these as our goals since the length of hospitalization permitted to her by her insurance policy prevented the kind of extensive work which would exacerbate and extend the psychotic state. The whole point of discussing goals is to emphasize the importance of establishing them as soon as possible in co-operation with staff and patients. Many therapists are accustomed to working with the luxury of extended and even unlimited time which is denied the therapeutic staff of most in-patient services. In order to avoid an amorphous, non-specific and unclear treatment experience, it is a must for the therapist to have early, clear-cut treatment goals, tentative as they may be.

The ultimate goal for *all* hospital groups is to make the experience one which the patient will want to continue upon his discharge. Too many therapists are unaware of how traumatic certain group experiences can be for hypersensitive schizophrenic patients. Upon their discharge it is often impossible to get a large number of them back into an after care therapy group. They refer back to certain hospital group experiences with terror and to others as a complete, boring waste of time.

The aim is to get the patient involved in a therapeutic process while still in the hospital, a process he will be willing and even desirous of continuing on an out-patient basis.

This is based upon the premise that for most patients only a part of the job can be done while they are in the hospital.

It is important for the therapist to identify the nature of the conflicts and stresses which produced the psychotic process and to help the patient contain that process. The therapist cannot, however, expect to resolve life-long problems in the short time alloted. For most patients an extended after-care program, with extensive use of groups is essential.

A different group approach is used for each category of patients. None of them are new and all have been used elsewhere.

For category A (patients with completely overwhelmed egos) an activity method is utilized. For category B (partially overwhelmed ego) a discussion technique is used and for the more intact patient a focal therapeutic approach is resorted to.

ACTIVITY GROUP

The activity group approach is divided into three parts: (1.) individual activity; (2.) diadic (pairs); (3.) group activity.

The purpose is to get the patients involved and interacting with each other. Neither exploration nor insight is sought. The aim is to help them know the staff and each other through engaging in an activity that is non-threatening and enjoyable. I call it a non-insight-supportive-relationship activity group. An activity is exploited to get everyone involved in a common group endeavor.

The group may start by working with finger painting or clay. (At Good Samaritan Hospital in Suffern, N.Y. at least 20 activities have been devised by the staff.) The group is told, "We would like to know you better and understand how you relate to yourselves and to each other. This is an exercise which increases self-awareness and by engaging in it you can help yourself and others." The first part engages the patient in a solo but parallel activity.

Typed instructions clearly explain the equipment that everyone is going to work with. All therapists participate fully in every phase of the work. If using finger paints the instructions read, "The jars are on the table, along with newspaper, paper cups, spatulas, wet paper, etc. Go up to the table and fill up several paper cups with the different colors you wish to use. Bring newspaper, cups, and the wet paper back to your place. Spread out the newspaper, put your wet paper down on top of it, etc." Before starting, one of the patients usually reads the instructions aloud.

Why written instructions? The aim is to utilize and exercise as many ego functions as possible. Some of the patients are still hallucinating, others delusional and some acutely depressed. Reading forces them to come into touch with an outside reality. (Patients often report that they have their most bizarre symptoms when they are alone and inactive.)

When they read the instructions they have to think about: where the paints are, what colors are there, etc. This immediately focuses their attention onto an outer reality. Intelligence must be exercised and they are forced into contact with their immediate surroundings. They are being asked to come out from their inner world and to perform a simple task.

No one is coerced into participating, although almost all do. Occasionally a particularly paranoid delusional person or an extremely terrified and fastidious patient will refuse. When they see all the others walking up to the table, getting their paints, sitting down and engaging in the activity, most grudgingly get involved. It is difficult for them to resist the flow of the group, although they may not do exactly what the others are doing and may remain isolated on the periphery. Those who won't engage at all are told that that is "fine." They can sit and watch and they are free to join in whenever they wish. (If a patient leaves the room a staff member goes out an encourages him to return. When a minimal degree of group cohesiveness is established the group is asked to handle the situation.) The non-active but observing patient is engaged by watching the others. His participation as a spectator is acceptable during this first solo part of the activity phase.

The first portion is dedicated to getting the patient out of himself and engaged in a simple non-threatening task, all by himself but near others. Patients usually start engaging in simple interactions i.e. "pass me a cup" or "I'll get that for you." They look at what their neighbor is doing and smile or frown. This parallel activity inevitably fosters this type of process.

After everyone, including staff, complete their pictures a minute is taken to explain what was painted and what it meant. (Sometimes everyone paints to music and relates the painting to what is heard.) Members often comment upon each other's work and all words of praise and encouragement by patients are rewarded by the leaders. This reenforcement of positive feelings between members is consciously used to foster group closeness. (Liberman, 1971). The reward for any positive patient interaction may consist of a simple, "That was nice of you to say that to Mary."

After the individual phase is completed the patients are asked to return to their instruction sheets. Here they are told to select a partner and to paint a picture together. This is often an easier operation because of the minimal interaction which occured during the solo part of the activity. This diadic activity forces patients to engage with another person in a structured, non-threatening and enjoyable activity. He has the opportunity to learn that simple interrelatedness and interaction can be fun and not full of pain and humiliation. This may enable him to take another step in relating with others.

The pair discusses and decides upon their common project and after they carry through on it the group discusses each pair's endeavors. Once again the aim is to encourage interaction and generate group cohesiveness.

In the last portion of the activity phase the entire group is instructed to engage in a common joint effort. They must all decide upon what they want to do. They have to determine who does what part of the project and then produce their masterpiece.

By this time the feeling emerges that these separate, isolated people belong to a group. There is usually a lot of laughter, encouragement, self-criticism, praise and disappointment, but it is a shared experience. There is discussion about how different people reacted and behaved and how they felt about the project and each other. Nothing profound is sought after and everyone's contribution is highly appreciated. The staff's full and even joyous participation is the key to success. When the staff sits by professionally detached and merely observes, the spontaneity and joy are noticably less, even absent, from the group.

This approach leads people into talking with each other and to discussing non-threatening areas. After a session or two, with most groups, the discussion has not been completed by the end of the session and it is at this point the therapist suggests that they continue it at the next session.

At the folowing session the group follows through on the topic that they had ended on. This follow-through from activity to discussion is not forced and usually comes about easily and naturally. At times, with a very regressed group, activity has to be resorted to again after the discussion is exhausted. This occurs more often on units in a mental hospital serving chronic long-term patients. The choice of what part of the activity (individual, diadic or group) to return to depends on the particular group.

With chronic patients who have been hospitalized for several years, it may be necessary to stay with an activity approach for several weeks, even months. With less damaged patients, the ego exercise received through the activity, plus the enormous decrease in anxiety due to drug therapy, removal from external stress (family) situations, plus rest, hot meals and sleep, all enable flooded ego capacities to emerge rather quickly. This frequently occurs due to the enormous decrease in the secondary anxiety level. Patients who experience bizarre symptoms for the first time are terrified by the realization that something strange is happening to them, something which they cannot control or comprehend. One patient who began seeing the devil one morning realized that, "I must be going crazy. I went into a total panic which made it even worse." The anxiety and terror generated by the person's awareness that a sick process is occurring tends to completely overwhelm remaining ego functions. Upon admission, such patients fit into category A. In a relatively short period of time, often from two days to one week, they are again able to reflect upon the psychotic process. This happens because the overall anxiety level is enormously decreased by drugs and a supportive and understanding treatment approach. At this point they fit into category B.

The group approach during this anxiety-decreasing period should not do anything to increase anxiety. With this in mind, the nature and sequence of the activity chosen should be explored.

Certain activities arouse more anxiety in patients than do others.

Dancing for example arouses more overt fear and resistance in patients than does working with clay or blocks. Any activity which requires people to touch each other should come later on in the group's life. This is also true for those activities which ask the patients to make up stories or to reveal personal life experiences.

Thus the purpose of the activity group approach is to enable terrified, suspicious and psychotic people to come near to each other, then through a structured method to enable them to start interacting. This will help some to seal over their psychotic symptoms and permit for early discharge and maintenance therapy. Most will move on into the discussion phase of the approach.

DISCUSSION GROUP TECHNIQUES

For those who have moved from category A into category B and those who entered with some non-psychotic ego capacity, a discussion group technique has evolved.

Ten to twelve patients sit around a table and are free to choose their own discussion topics. The table is used to avoid immediate intimacy which usually raises the anxiety level. Topics are broad and general and people are allowed to be non-specific and non-personal. The therapist may suggest certain themes to start off with such as: What usually annoys people about others? How does it feel to be a patient? How do we usually deal with angry feelings? What usually stops people from expressing strong emotions? etc.

These themes are clearly related to the kinds of problems that brought most of them into the hospital, yet no one is forced, coerced or confronted to be personal, intimate or even to speak in the first person. General global statements are accepted and any participation is encouraged and rewarded.

What frequently happens is that people don't listen to each other and bring up totally unrelated material. Nonsequitors abound, eight people talk at once and all statements are directed at the therapist. People want to know about medication, discharge and visits; patients try to have one-to-one sessions with the staff leader, and if more than one therapist is present each may be approached separately, with three separate interviews going on at the same time. People want to leave. Comments are made only to the nearest neighbors and the leaders keep trying heroically to keep everyone on the agreed-upon topic. At times it makes a three ring circus seem a quiet and pleasant affair. This happens most frequently when category A patients are mistakenly in the group and during the beginning phase of the discussion experience.

I prefer to preface the meeting by outlining the purpose and methods very clearly. I may open the session with, "We are here today to talk about topics which are of interest and concern to all of us. Everyone should make a serious attempt to contribute his thoughts. You may be scared or think that your ideas are unimportant. They are not. They may be useful to someone in the group. At the same time try to give your fellow group members a chance to speak, too. One thing we have all learned from life is that people seldom *really* listen to each other. They either interrupt or else are thinking about what they are going to say while the other person is still talking. Let us try to be different and really try to listen. Then try and honestly respond to what you heard. This is the least we can do for each other and it often turns out to be very helpful."

A group may spend a week or even two on general discussions. The leader sums up the general ideas and themes and conceptualizes broad mental health concepts. After the first week the leader may encourage people to speak in the first person and directly to others. He may also ask for specific examples which underly the generalizations, i.e. "Could you tell the group how this actually applies to your life?"

This cannot be pressed too hard nor too soon. The leader must take his cues from the group. One or two members usually start it off on their own and the leader then helps others to do the same.

An interesting phenomenon occurs after a period of speaking in general terms. Certain members know that they are soon leaving the hospital. They also know that they have not been discussing their personal problems. Such phrases as, "I don't feel this group is getting down to the real source or core of our problems" or "we never get down to the nitty gritty" or "this is all very nice, but it isn't really going to help me when I leave."

It is at this point that the group is asking for and is ready for a different group therapy approach. Groups give their cues and a sensitive leader can hear them and respond accordingly. A major advantage of these first two approaches is that skillful clinicians are not necessary, Outside of large cities and teaching hospitals few experienced therapists are available to conduct these groups several times a week. The work can be done by beginning social workers, experienced nurses and occupational and recreational therapists. Trained aides and other mature paraprofessionals have conducted these groups with great success and with minimal supervision.

FOCAL THERAPY

Membership is open to those from category C and those from category B whose ego resources have strengthened and recuperated during their stay and are now ready for a more insightful approach to their problems. Quite often, a discussion group which had evolved from an activity group progresses into a focal therapy group. It does not tend to occur rapidly with chronic long-term patients but most frequently happens in a short-term unit with a general hospital or a short-term private hospital. Needless to say, a state hospital serves a very different patient population than does a small unit in a suburban or rural community. Our society still sends its poorest and most damaged members to its out-of-sight-out-of-mind institutions.

In focal therapy the focus is limited to: (1.) what precipitated the acute pathological response which necessitated hospitalization; (2.) what the immediate conflicts were that produced the pathological reaction; (3.) hew they dealt with it; (4.) how their maladaptive patterns emerge on the ward and especially in the group in the here and how; (5.) and finally to the discovery of alternate modes of behavior which they can practice and which can be rewarded and reinforced while still in the hospital.

It is not the therapist's intention to resolve completely these conflicts but rather to identify them and to engage the patient in working upon them. The aim is to involve him in a therapeutic process which he will be willing if not eager to continue upon his discharge.

When the past is explored it is only in relation to the patients' specific present day conflicts and care is taken not to uncover at random past conflicts, pains, traumas and anxieties. When the past is discussed it is directly linked, in a clear way, to how it is influencing present-day functioning.

If possible the focus remains upon the immediate precipitating factors which evoked the maladaptive response. John, 41, married, three children, was admitted because of a depression. He had been on the surgical ward for major surgery a few weeks earlier and a few weeks after discharge became depressed. He was constantly concerned about his wife whom he feared could not manage while he was away. He had suffered a depression eight years before. It soon became clear that his wife had been telling him her problems and fears while he was awaiting surgery and during his recuperation. She had expected *him* to look after *her* needs even though he very much needed to be taken care of himself. Her blindness to his realistic needs was obvious to everyone but him.

Instead of asserting his own needs he kept worrying about her and began to feel guilty about being sick. "What is she going to do without me, her mother is going home in a few days and she will be alone."

In the group, members pointed out how unrealistic he was about himself. He was the one that needed to be cared for and his wife was quite able to manage by herself. In fact, after all these years, if they had a real partnership, she ought to be looking after him. Other members expressed great anger at his wife. John, protective of her, was able to admit a slight annoyance at her.

The patient was unaware of the degree of his rage at his infantile and demanding mate. His reactive depression was due to a general weakening of ego strength due to the recent major surgery. The surgery affected his self and body image and also deprived him of his compulsive work activities which served as an adequate defense against rage. Deprived of this, his rage was turned against himself and emerged as depression. We judged the rage to be homocidal in nature, especially after surgery. We speculated that his wife was similar to his mother whom he also looked after until her death. We were not interested in making that connection and stayed in the present and supported his right to be annoyed. On the floor and in the group we highlighted again and again how he could not express anger at anyone. We questioned the reasons for this, since it was clear to the entire group that this was a problem.

We attempted to help him assert himself on the floor and rewarded any slight sign of it. He gradually began to speak up rather tenuously.

We wanted to make the connection between his sense of being burdened and depression with his feelings about the constant demands made upon him by his wife. We considered in the group why he felt he had to do everything for her. That was not required nor was it good for her. She had to use and exercise her own strengths and assets. His babying her made her weaker, not stronger. In eight days his depression lifted. He felt stronger, asked for couple therapy on an outpatient basis and wanted to continue in group therapy.

In this instance, the goals were quite limited and focused. We identified the immediate noxious source, focused in on it; helped him to see how unexpressed affects can boomerang; and encouraged and reinforced an alternative form of behavior which he then practiced on the floor and in the group.

Whether or not patients tell us what they think their problems are, they invariably demonstrate, in the group, the pathological behavior patterns which underlie their disturbance. The experienced therapist is bombarded by these communications which the patient cannot express in any other way than to enact them for the therapist in his relation to group members. The therapist, if he can, points out these maladaptive patterns and shows how they work against the patient, both in the group and in his everyday life.

These focal therapy groups are smaller in size than the activity and discussion groups—usually from six to eight patients. A senior member of the staff with more extensive clinical experience usually conducts them. It is hard to keep goals in view and to work only in selected areas and untrained therapists tend to wander, allow for too much uncovering and find it difficult to detect repetitive maladaptive patterns.

The experience has to be crisp and exciting. The therapist identifies the problem and gets the patients involved in working on them. In the final phase, outpatient treatment plans are discussed and arranged and, if possible, the patient starts attending his outpatient group while still in the hospital. It is important that the inpatient group be involved in helping the patient get involved in his outpatient treatment.

As one young woman stated, "At least I know now what the hell is bothering me and I know what I have to work on. Although I'm going to be afraid to start, I'm going to." Since she was going to return to another city the staff could not follow through completely, but did find a therapist for her and spoke to him. If she did not contact him they were to be informed. They never heard from him and assumed she did follow through.

Over all, groups are used to make the hospital stay pleasant, exciting and rewarding. A therapeutic milieu is supplied which gives the drug therapy a chance to work. People often think it is the other way around. but it is not. Some staffs immobilize their patients on high dosages in order to manage them. I find that the therapeutic group approach helps to manage the patient so that he can be treated with more reasonable dosage levels which do not make him a walking zombie. Groups can be used to bring the patient out of his emotional isolation and withdrawal and into contact and relations with other human beings.

A medium is offered in which he can learn and practice different modes of relating and get some idea of how he affects other people. The therapist focuses on how the patient unwittingly alienates and antagonizes others and how he deals with his major emotions, such as anger, tenderness and hurt.

This is started during the end phase of the discussion group and centered upon during focal therapy. The entire staff is used, all through the day and night, to help the patient practice less self-destructive ways of expressing his affects. This is discussed in the group and the patients cooperation is enlisted in determining what behavior he wishes to alter. Therapy is thus an all day process which is formulated in the group and carried on by every staff member through all of the shifts. Fellow group members are even more important because they are involved in helping each other alter the maladaptive patterns which were revealed in the group sessions and they encourage each other throughout the day to practice the new patterns that were suggested in the group.

A deep sense of community begins to develop where warmth, support and camaraderie are much in evidence. One very withdrawn and suspicious man, George, age 46, could say after ten days, "You know, this is the first time in my life that I have ever spoken like this in front of a group. I had to bring myself up since I was a little boy. My father died when I was three and I was the oldest. I never let anybody help me. It was always, 'George could always do it for himself. George knows how.' Shit, George didn't know beans and I am only beginning to realize that now. It's the first time I've expressed anything about myself to anybody. You know what? It feels great!"

For the therapist, the approaches discussed above are rewarding and difficult. Often patients remain in the activity or discussion phase of the work. Sometimes there are not enough people to form a focal therapy group. With very damaged patients there is either no or very little opportunity during a short hospitalization to work with them in focal therapy because by the time they are ready for it they are also ready for discharge.

On many psychiatric wards therapists immediately attempt to use focal insight therapy with acutely psychotic (category A) patients. The therapist then finds himself coping with all kinds of management problems since this approach can stimulate levels of anxiety which this category of patient cannot tolerate without resorting to extreme fight-flight reactions and bizarre psychotic behavior.

The patient who is still struggling with an active psychosis does not want to talk about the causes of his problems. This patient will say, "I don't want to talk about my real problem because it upsets me too much and it doesn't help me. I can't deal with it." This is told verbally to the therapist whom the patient knows and trusts. When the therapist is a stranger, the patient will say the same thing through behavior. He will run out of the room, not be on the ward for the next meeting, become agitated and violent during and after the group session, withdraw into sleep or bizarre behavior, go "awol" or as a last resort commit suicide.

The therapist who insists in working in an uncovering way with such patients finds himself dealing with these problems and he has to decide such issues as: Should we lock and bar the door? Should we prohibit (using physical force if necessary) any patient from leaving the session? Should we lock up the ward so as to prevent patients from leaving before sessions? How are we going to deal with a resentful staff which has to live with the agitated and violent reactions? Should we use high levels of medication to restrain violent and agitated behavior during and after the sessions?

If the above approach is to be used successfully the therapist must have a considerable body of experience and skill and thoroughly train and involve his staff so that they can tolerate and actively support this approach. In many cases this is unfeasible, since most hospitals have under-manned and under-trained staffs.

An approach which is more acceptable to me is one which recognizes the enormous anxiety and pain the schizophrenic patient is struggling with. The schizophrenic patient must be approached at a pace he can tolerate and which does not threaten him with complete loss of control. A healthy respect for his defenses and the reasons for them is essential.

Therapists may become impatient in their desire to help as much as possible in the short time alloted and thus use methods which may be unintentionally hurtful. Unfortunately a myth exists in the field that the only "real therapy" is insight therapy and anything else such as activity or discussion is for those who are low on the hierarchical totem pole. This has proven disastrous for the severely disturbed patient since the more experienced and trained professional will not deign to engage in a treatment approach which is below his dignity but is never the less the kind of treatment which may be best for the patient. The experienced therapist often has little experience or skill utilizing activity or theme centered approaches and thus does not use them. He instead attempts to do what he is most familiar and comfortable with which often proves unhelpful and even hurtful to the still psychotic patient.

The therapist in a very short-term group psychotherapy approach which I have presented can never reach the working through stage of treatment. He is always in the beginning formation and first stage of group therapy, and gets the patients prepared for ongoing therapy with someone else. It can be and is frustrating for those who like to see things through to the end and it is a repetitive and endless job. The complete turnover of patients almost every two weeks keeps the staff at the beginning of the process. If they are to be successful the staff must become involved, committed and deeply concerned. They then have to separate from the people they have come to care about and this chronic separation makes short-term in-patient group psychotherapy a painful job, especially for the neophyte therapist.

SUMMARY

It is clear that what this approach attempts to do is establish a therapeutic regimen with acutely ill patients. Group methods are used to diminish the anxiety associated with self-exposure before others. Structured situations are utilized to control the anxiety level of the group. Since confrontation and non-directive approaches stimulate high degrees of tension and anxiety it is this author's belief that they should be avoided in a short-term setting. This does not rule out eventual forms of confrontation or non-directive approaches. My approach aims to establish a treatment relationship which can tolerate and fully utilize these approaches if they are indicated with particular patients. My major concern is that we take care not to alienate patients from the treatment process which many of them need to continue when they leave hospital care. The fight against a psychotic process is often a lifetime battle and group approaches are proving very valuable in helping many people to remain free of psychosis for longer periods of time.

References

Lieberman, R. (1971): Reinforcement of Cohesiveness in Group Therapy. *Archives of General Psychiatry*, **25** (2), 168–177.

Suggested readings

Bellak, L. and Small, L. (1965): *Emergency Psychotherapy and Brief Psychotherapy*, New York, Grune and Stratton.

Frank, J. D. (1963): Group Therapy in the Mental Hospital. In M. Rosenbaum, M. Berger (Eds.), *Group Psychotehrapy and Group Function*, New York ,Basic Books, 477–486.

Wolf, A. (1965): Short-Term Group Psychotherapy. In Wolberg, L. R. (Ed.), *Short-Term Psychotherapy*, New York, Grune and Stratton, 219–255.

About the authors

Samuel B. hadden is Associate Professor of Psychiatry, Emeritus, of the University of Pennsylvania School of Medicine. He is a fellow of the AGPA (American Group Psychotherapy Association), has written scores of articles in psychiatry and neurology, and has been in private practice for many years.

Herbert M. Rabin is on the editorial board of GROUP PROCESS. He is in private practice and is Director of Group Therapy Training, Blanton-Peale Graduate Institute. He is also supervisor and training analyst in Analytic Group Psychotherapy at the Postgraduate Center For Mental Health, and Clinical Professor of Psychology, Postdoctoral Program in Psychotherapy, Adelphi University. He has written extensively in psychotherapy, especially group therapy.

Max Rosenbaum is editor of GROUP PROCESS. He is in private practice and has been visiting professor at the City University. He is clinical professor, Adelphi University. He is also president of Human Resources Development and Conservation Corporation and author of books and many articles in the field of group psychotherapy. He lectures in the USA as well as Europe and South America.

James M. Sacks is director of the Moreno Institute (for psychodrama) and in the private practice of psychocherapy and psychodrama. He is past president of the Society of Group Therapy and Psychodrama.

Edward M. Scott is Clinic Director of the Oregon State Alcohol and Drug Treatment Center, and Associate Clinical Professor of Psychiatry at the University of Oregon Medical School. In addition to two recent books, one on alcoholism and the other on happiness, he has written widely on group therapy and alcoholism.

Dorothy Stock Whitaker is currently Professor of Social Work at the University of York in England. Previously she taught in the

Psychology Department of the University of Chicago. Her writing in group therapy has included one basic text and numerous articles.

Isaac Zeke Youcha is Assistant Clinical Professor in the Department of Psychiatry at the Albert Einstein College of Medicine and in private practice. He is a graduate of the Postgraduate Center for Mental Health where he trained in Psychotherapy and Psychoanalysis and in Analytic Group Psychotherapy.

For Product Safety Concerns and Information please contact our EU representative GPSR@taylorandfrancis.com
Taylor & Francis Verlag GmbH, Kaufingerstraße 24, 80331 München, Germany

www.ingramcontent.com/pod-product-compliance
Ingram Content Group UK Ltd.
Pitfield, Milton Keynes, MK11 3LW, UK
UKHW021507240926
475702UK00035B/653
* 9 7 8 1 1 3 8 8 0 1 3 9 4 *